THE SPIRITUAL
FOUNDATIONS
OF AIKIDO

■ *Morihei Ueshiba, the founder of aikido. Photo courtesy of Mitsugi Saotome-sensei, Aikido Schools of Ueshiba.*

THE
SPIRITUAL
FOUNDATIONS
OF
AIKIDO

WILLIAM GLEASON

DESTINY BOOKS
Rochester, Vermont

■

Destiny Books
One Park Street
Rochester, Vermont 05767
Web Site: http://www.gotoit.com

LIBRARY OF CONGRESS CATALOGING-IN-PUBLICATION DATA
Gleason, William, 1943–
The spiritual foundations of aikido / William Gleason.
p.   cm.
Includes bibliographical references and index.
ISBN 0-89281-508-6
1. Aikido—Psychological aspects. I. Title
GV1114.35.G54   1994
796.8'154—dc20   94-26938
CIP

Printed and bound in the United States

10   9   8   7   6   5   4   3

Art and illustrations by Cynthia Zoppa
Calligraphy by Hisako Gleason
Technical photography by Missy Harvey
Ukemi for technical photos by Warren Stanley and Rick Santos
Text design and layout by Virginia L. Scott
This book was typeset in Optima with Letter Gothic as display type

Calligraphy on half title and title pages,
Shido: Japanese Kototama Scholar (1765–1843), by Michio Hikitsuchi sensei,
wakayama prefecture, Japan.

Destiny Books is a division of Inner Traditions International

Distributed to the book trade in Canada by Publishers Group West (PGW),
Toronto, Ontario

Distributed to the book trade in the United Kingdom by Deep Books, London

Distributed to the book trade in Australia by Millennium Books, Newtown, N.S.W.

Distributed to the book trade in New Zealand by Tandem Press, Auckland

Distributed to the book trade in South Africa by Alternative Books, Randburg

■

CONTENTS

推薦の辞

　　　古今の歴史の発展を考える時一人の
人間の努力と情熱と創造力に負うところが
多大であるというが、今般、私の長年の友人
であり合氣道の良き指導者でもあります。
ビル・グリソン氏によって「合氣道、精神的礎」
という本がINNER, TRADITIONS出版社
より出版されることは合氣道の人々だけでは
なく古来の日本の宗教、芸術、武術等の理解を
得たいと思う人々にとっても非常に参考になるもの
と存じます。合氣道開祖、植芝大先生も
江のほかに「言霊ことだま」と合氣道の奥義
について教示されていたが、ビル・グリソン氏
の努力と研究が世に出て、合氣道の修業
者に良き参考書になるものと期待致します。

6. 20. 1993

合氣道師範　亜月女貢

A WORD OF RECOMMENDATION

WHEN WE REFLECT ON THE DEVELOPMENTS of past history, we owe a considerable debt of gratitude to certain men and women who, through undaunted effort, determination, and creativity, have made exceptional contributions. Such may be said of Bill Gleason, who is my longtime friend and a highly qualified instructor of aikido.

The Spiritual Foundations of Aikido is not only of interest for those people studying aikido, but is also a valuable resource for anyone wishing more deeply to understand ancient Japanese religion, fine art, and martial art.

Morihei Ueshiba-sensei, the founder of aikido, emphatically stressed the relevance of the kototama to the secret principle, or essence, of aikido, and I have every anticipation that this book, the result of Bill Gleason's long effort and research, will find its place as a well of information for those who study aikido.

Mitsugi Saotome, Aikido Shihan
June 20, 1993

ACKNOWLEDGMENTS

DURING THE TWENTY-SEVEN YEARS OF MY spiritual odyssey, I have had the good fortune to be influenced by some of the most gifted teachers in the world. This book is an attempt to share some of the wealth that I have received. I understand that concepts cannot convey the reality of that which has been experienced directly, yet without words we cannot even begin the journey toward meaningful communication. With this consolation in mind, I have undertaken the writing of this book.

It is impossible to list all the people who have helped me; I will mention only the main influences, in the order that they appeared in my life. Michio Kushi, leader of the world macrobiotic movement, who first introduced me to the idea that there is a universal law and order and that we can control our own destiny. Master Seigo Yamaguchi, disciple of the founder, Morihei Ueshiba, and whose incredible genius continues to inspire my practice today. Yoshinobu Takeda, highest student of Yamaguchi Sensei, and founder of the Shonan Aikido Federation and the world Cultural Development Center (CDC). Takeda Sensei picked me up when I was down and has continued to help and teach me ever since. Without his support and teaching I can't imagine how I ever would have succeeded with my Aikido studies in Japan. Mitsugi Saotome Shihan, disciple of the Ueshiba Morihei and founder of Aikido Schools of Ueshiba (ASU). Without Saotome Sensei's continual support and encouragement the dream of this book would not have become a reality. Finally I cannot forget the many evenings spent around the Japanese kotatsu (heat lamp table) at the home of Sanae Odano in Tokyo, listening to her wonderful teachings of the kototama. Odano Sensei's dedication, wisdom, and vision concerning the meaning of human life fills my heart, even now, with fond memories.

A NOTE TO THE READER

Pronunciation

A———as in father
E———as in save
I———as in easy
O———as in old
U———as in smooth
Si is pronounced *Shi.*
Ti is pronounced *Chi.*
Tu is pronounced *Tsu.*
R is pronounced as a combination of the English *r*, *l*, and *d* sounds. It is similar to a Spanish *r* but is not rolled.

Glossary

A Glossary of terms used is provided at the back of the book. In some cases, foreign words and technical terms are explained in text; in other cases, not. Readers will sometimes wish to turn to the Glossary.

INTRODUCTION

INTEREST IN THE MARTIAL ARTS IN THE WEST has been increasing in the last decade, yet many people still do not understand that there is a major difference between the martial arts, as they are commonly practiced and portrayed, and *budo*, the martial way. *Budo*, or simply *bu*, is a shortened form of the word *bushido*, the traditional philosophy and way of life underlying the conduct and training of the Japanese samurai warrior. Budo encompasses both the martial and the fine arts; it nurtures both aesthetic appreciation and practical ability. The code of bushido has defined the standard for traditional education in Japan for many centuries, instilling in the Japanese people a sense of justice, courage, morality, and benevolence. I believe that this makes it particularly valuable for our modern times. It is, in fact, already having a large influence on Western society, and it is important that we understand its true nature.

Regardless of the purity or depth of the ancient martial arts, as long as modern adaptations emphasize formal competition as their raison d'être, they are sports, not budo. The competitive aspect of the martial arts has been escalated by misinformed and misleading publicity generated by popular magazines and movies. It is my intention in *The Spiritual Foundations of Aikido* to situate aikido within its true budo heritage and to establish its value as a spiritual discipline. Aikido is unique among martial disciplines in that its ingenious design allows it to be practiced with full bodily contact *without injury or competition*.

Aikido is a modern form of budo that embodies the essence of Shinto, the indigenous religion and spiritual foundation of Japan. Shinto mind is, in fact, Japanese mind. The original Shinto *(kannagara no michi)* precedes religion: it is a tradition older than written history. It is at the heart of bu, a way of life based on a worldview that underlies the samurai code of social responsibility. The Japanese sword—essential to the higher refinement of aikido technique and central to aikido history—is one of the three sacred symbols of Shinto.

Shinto and aikido are tied together by their common foundation, the *kototama* principle. The kototama principle manifests universal energy *(ki)*. The kototama (word souls—see chapter 4) divides this *ki* into fifty different functions that underlie all phenomena. These word souls are sounds—but not merely sounds as we usually think of them. They are the a priori dimensions of the universe manifesting through the eight different rhythms of yin and yang (see Glossary). They are the foundation of our spiritual constitution—in fact, of the whole universe. The techniques of aikido were created in accordance with this principle; and aikido, practiced with the correct mentality, leads to spiritual understanding and personal transformation.

This is not a book on aikido technique per se. Rather, it is an attempt to introduce the principles that lie at the root of that technique. The founder of aikido, Morihei Ueshiba-sensei, described the essence of aikido as *One Spirit, Four Souls, Three Origins, and Eight Powers.* This is the Shinto expression for the kototama principle. O-sensei went on to say that if our practice departed from this principle, we were missing aikido altogether. It is my intention in this book to clarify these original teachings of aikido through the teachings of Shinto from which they originate.

Where I quote O-sensei's direct teachings, I specify them as such, and they are printed in italic type. In all other cases I draw on my own research and experience. It is not my intention to explain the kototama in depth but, rather, to clarify its basic principles and reveal the spiritual content of aikido.

Each chapter of this book builds on the one before, and I therefore recommend that they be read in order. Having read the entire text once through, the reader may then return and study specific points of interest.

Chapter 1 introduces the life of the founder, Morihei Ueshiba-sensei, and the experiences that led to his unique ability and spiritual enlightenment. It introduces the unique sword training that led to his depth of spiritual conviction and dedication to world peace. Some of his aikido poems are also introduced.

Chapter 2 deals with the spiritual qualities of aikido. Various Japanese terms are introduced to show its philosophical and experiential content as well as the proper attitude for practice.

Chapter 3 introduces the cosmology of *kannagara no michi*, the original Shinto, and also the mythology that has been passed down to the present. The kototama are introduced as the foundation of both Shinto and Japanese mind. It was through O-sensei's study of the kototama, Shinto, and esoteric Buddhism that the creation of aikido became possible.

In chapter 4 the kototama are approached as the content of universal order, the world of ki. This chapter is not easy reading, but it explains the thread that unites *The Spiritual Foundations of Aikido* and should be read carefully. The origin of the five vowel dimensions is explained as emptiness, which is said to be the reality of all consciousness and form. The three sacred treasures of Shinto—the mirror, the sword, and the beads—are related to their respective kototama.

Chapter 5 introduces the theme of One Spirit, Four Souls, the constitution of both individual and universal spirit. This is an aspect of spirituality that is little known in the West and it is the foundation of O-sensei's spiritual teachings.

Chapter 6 deals with spiritual manifestation: the Three Origins and Eight Powers, the foundation of both religion and philosophy.

Chapter 7 explains the need for practice and goes on to unite the universal principles of *aiki,* the harmony of universal ki, with actual technique and practice. The purpose of aikido practice is to understand the aiki principle and apply it to every aspect of our lives. Aikido technique can never really be correct until we become one with the laws of harmony in nature.

Chapter 8, "The Order of the Universe," concerns the application of aiki principle and feeling to our daily life. It is a call to consciousness, a request for all aikido people to unite and support the dream of O-sensei: the creation of a better world.

I was one of many young people, who, in the early 1960s, were searching for some of the answers to the question, Why do we exist? It was a time when many people were trying, like snakes, to change their skin—and trying to discover something, anything, that made sense. This search led me to Boston, Massachusetts, where I became a student of Michio Kushi, the founder of the U.S. macrobiotic movement. His teachings on universal order and the wisdom of the East so inspired me that I became a teacher, lecturing and traveling in the United States. Several years later, as though finding the answer to a question I had not known how to ask, I discovered aikido, a means of intuitively grasping the principles I had been studying. In December 1969 I left for Japan to study aikido in depth.

I studied with the best teachers in the world. My combined studies of Japanese language, Eastern religion, and aikido also led me to the roots of Japanese culture, the kototama. The kototama is the content and function of universal and individual spirit. Aikido, constructed on its form and function, embodies this origin and makes it available for anyone to discover through his or her own effort.

In the spring of 1980 I returned to the United States to continue training and also to teach. This martial way has become the center of my life. My dojo is named Shobu Aikido of Boston. *Shobu* means the martial way of wisdom. It indicates that aikido must be practiced as *michi*—as a total way of life. Shobu aikido brings forth the virtues of One Spirit, Four Souls, the five vowel dimensions of the universe. I am not a master of aikido; I am a student on the path. As such it is my sincere wish that this book will be read with an open mind and be of value to those who seek a better understanding of the spiritual content of aikido.

The Path of Shobu Aiki

真	U	sincerity and self-reflection
愛	A	mercy and compassion
美	O	beauty and self-organization
善	E	judgment and courage
智	I	wisdom and self-control

---

1 ■ THE ORIGINS OF AIKIDO

ALTHOUGH IT IS MOST WIDELY KNOWN as a martial art or system of self-defense, aikido is also a profound spiritual training. Its purpose is to develop the innate qualities of our divine heritage. This was the opinion stated by aikido's founder, Morihei Ueshiba (1883–1969), a Japanese soldier, farmer, and philosopher, and one of the greatest martial arts masters in history. In recognition of his contribution to the martial arts, aikido practitioners refer to him as O-sensei, "the great teacher." As created and fashioned by O-sensei, aikido's purpose is to promote life and understanding, not to defeat others. The only enemy that Ueshiba recognized was the enemy within.

His final message to his students before he passed away was that the name of aikido should be changed to *shobu aiki*, the martial way for the creation of wisdom and character. These were his words:

> The martial way [budo] *that embodies the feeling of universal compassion is based on the creative energy of the universe* [takemusubi]. *All the others are nothing more than arts of destruction. In the beginning I called it* takemusubi aiki; *later I decided to call it* shobu aiki, *the budo that creates wisdom, judgment, the mind of a sage.*[1]

■ *Morihei Ueshiba*

> The true victory of shobu aiki is to strike down and destroy the mind of doubt and conflict within yourself. It is to realize and carry out the destiny you have received from divine providence. Regardless of how this may be philosophically explained, unless it is actually put into practice, you are no different than anyone else. Through the practice of aikido, this power and ability is added unto you.

■ *Shobu aiki*

The underlying origin of budo is the spirit of universal protection, nurturing, and salvation. It is to give renewed energy to yourself and others. Human beings are the children of the divine universal spirit and if they are unhappy it is because they turn away from their own nature. Man has selfishly created the sense of good and evil and then forgotten the essence of his own nature. Within divine love there is no good or evil, no happiness or unhappiness. There is only constant giving in an attempt to pay back some part of the precious gift of life that one has received and even now continues to enjoy.

You should never be trapped by the idea that you have problems, that you are a person of deep karma, or that you are one of little value. This is insulting not only to yourself but to others as well. All people share the same divine origin. There is only one thing that is wrong or useless. That is the stubborn insistence that you are an individual, separate from others. Give thanks and show gratitude. Work for the paradise on this earth. In this way your true nature will continually unfold.

These quotations are teachings of Morihei Ueshiba, born on December 14, 1883, in the village of Tanabe, near the sacred Nachi Falls, Wakayama prefecture, Japan. The area is deeply immersed in Shinto mysticism, esoteric Buddhism, and tales of ancient times. These stories influenced the young Morihei a great deal. He was the fourth child of Yoroku and Yuki Ueshiba, and his father went to great lengths in order to insure the happiness and success of his only son. Yoroku reputedly never raised his voice to young Ueshiba. His mother Yuki was a gentle and soft-spoken woman whose interests were in painting, calligraphy, literature, and religion. Between them, Morihei was exposed to both the martial and the fine arts at an early age.

Morihei, a sensitive child, was often ill. He had an introspective nature and spent much of his time reading and daydreaming. At seven years of age, he began studying at a local Buddhist temple of the Shingon Mikkyo sect and learned to chant the sacred mantras and scriptures of esoteric Buddhism.

The Shingon Mikkyo (lit., the secret teaching of the true word) sect was founded by the Buddhist saint Kobo-daishi (774–835 c.e.), also known as Kukai. Among other things, Kukai's talents were said to include the ability to paint four murals simultaneously by holding brushes in both his hands and feet. When Shingon Mikkyo became mixed with unsystemetized shamanism, the result was Shugendo, an ascetic mountain religion that linked this esoteric Buddhist sect with Shinto. Ueshiba wrote:

> *The esoteric Buddhism of Kukai, though incomparably more complex and sophisticated than Shinto, had many elements compatible with the latter. Among these were the idea of the oneness of man and nature and a belief in the magical efficacy of the word (mantra in the former, kototama in the latter). It was only natural that as time went by esoteric Buddhism should come into close association with Shinto.* [2]

Shingon gave the young Morihei his first introduction to the kototama as a spiritual practice. Chanting the Shingon incantations—the word souls—he showed great interest and aptitude, and his mother considered he might become a monk. His father, however, opposed. The idea died a peaceful death.

Yoroku Ueshiba, of samurai stock, was a man of considerable strength, and he encouraged his son to develop himself through the practice of sumo wrestling and swimming. Morihei was obliged to help his father every day, carrying heavy bags of rice and accompanying him on long mountainside excursions to visit hidden shrines and on trips to the seaside for fishing. In time, Morihei developed into a robust and healthy young man, but not so strong that he could handle anything that came up.

One evening when everyone was asleep, a gang of thieves broke into the house; Yoroku grabbed a staff, sending them running for their lives. Morihei recalled this event wistfully: "I wished at that time that I could have helped my father. I didn't know what to do." Perhaps this was the spark that in later years would kindle his desire to become a martial artist.

Morihei at first had no such intention. He was a bright student, avidly interested in mathematics and physics. After junior high school he enrolled in a highly regarded abacus academy and within a year became assistant to the instructor of the school. After graduating from the academy, Morihei took a job with the local tax office. He had a

■ *Shingon mikkyo*

quick mind and exceptional ability with figures and was rapidly promoted to superintendent.

His social conscience was evident early. When he was nineteen, a new law was imposed on fishermen, favoring the large commercial fleets and imposing hardship on the owners of small fishing boats. Morihei and the fishermen demonstrated against the law in what was known as the Iso Incident. This ended his career with the tax office. Jobless, but still the dreamer, he went north to Tokyo to seek his fortune and established the Ueshiba Company, which became a large stationery store. In the meantime he had become interested in the martial arts and studied both ancient *(koryu)* jujutsu and the *shinkage* style of Japanese sword. When later he became ill, he was forced to surrender his business to his employees and return home to Tanabe. Arriving, he said to his father, "Well, I left empty-handed and I returned empty-handed." Once again among familiar surroundings and eating well, he rapidly regained his health. In 1904 he married his childhood friend, Hatsu Itokawa.

In that same year, war broke out between Russia and Japan. Morihei enlisted in the army but was rejected for being a fraction under the minimum height requirement of five feet. This infuriated him. Eager to serve his country, he trained vigorously, alone in the mountains, and even hung for long periods of time by his arms from tree branches, hoping to stretch his height.

With his second application he was accepted as a reserve. His hardworking attitude and extraordinary skill soon drew the attention of his superiors, and he was quickly promoted to sergeant. His skill with both the sword and the bayonet guaranteed his promotion, yet the same skill kept him—against his wishes—off the battlefield: he was not sent to fight because he was considered too valuable as a teacher for other soldiers. When after repeated requests he was eventually sent to the front lines, he amazed his comrades by running directly into the attack. He claimed that when close enough, he could see the path of the enemy's bullets—a flash of light just before the bullet arrived. The bullet, he said, would follow the path of that light and if he dodged the flash of light, the bullet would miss him. This was the first evidence people had of his extrasensory ability.

Morihei's experiences in the war clearly established his direction toward martial arts. He came to know his opponent's every move before it was made. When threatened, he became even more calm, which thoroughly unsettled his opponents. His bravery and successful encounters on the battlefield made him a living legend, and he was respectfully called, "the soldier god." When the war ended in 1905, Morihei was offered the opportunity to enter the prestigious Toyama officers' school for professional soldiers. He probably would have done so had it not been for his father's request that his only son return to civilian life.

In 1907, at the age of twenty-four, Morihei returned home, full of doubts and confusion. He no longer had any interest in the business world, and due to his father's wishes he had abandoned his career as a soldier. He became moody and depressed, waking up in the middle of the night to pour cold water over himself. Sometimes he was angry for no apparent reason and would spend days in his room chanting Shinto prayers to calm himself. Without a word to anyone, he sometimes departed for the mountains to pray and fast, staying for weeks at a time.

Yoroku, concerned about his son's state of mind, cleared a space in his home and built a dojo—practice place—for Morihei. Shortly thereafter, Yoroku convinced Kiyoichi Takagi, a famous master of Kodokan judo who was traveling in the area, to come to the dojo and teach. Morihei had received a certificate from the Yagyu school of swordsmanship while in the army and had continued to train himself in that style after his discharge, receiving a teaching license in 1908. Takagi's arrival introduced him to modern judo, and he threw himself into it with a passion. He became happy again and even stronger than he had been in his military days.

During this period, Morihei studied judo every day. He also continued to train himself in swordsmanship, spear, and hard styles of jujutsu. He became so strong that he could split tree stumps with a wooden mallet and uproot young trees with his bare hands.

In 1912 the Japanese government, searching for additional living space for the population, announced the beginning of the Hokkaido project, encouraging people to settle in Japan's undeveloped northernmost island. The Russians, too, were showing an interest in Hokkaido's strategic location. There was little opportunity for either farming or fishing in Tanabe, and Morihei, like other dissatisfied veterans of the Russo-Japanese War, was eager to try a new adventure and also to be

▪ *Judo*

■ *Daito-ryu*

of further service to Japan. After some debate, Morihei, with his wife, Hatsu, led fifty-four families into the wilderness of Hokkaido.

The land was inhospitable and winter storms made the new settlers' makeshift housing little better than useless. The price in human suffering and sickness was high. Some people died due to the harsh environment and many families left. Morihei's optimism, hard work, and encouragement kept the remaining families going through these hardships, and they eventually carved out a new community near the village of Shirataki. Out of the wilderness they created farms, raised horses, and started a lumbering business.

Morihei stood out from the rest. The period bore witness to his physical strength, iron will, peacefulness of mind, and growing intuition. Once, on a surveying trip into the forest when he reputedly startled a bear that was searching for food, he calmed the bear with his confident manner. His charisma and extraordinary abilities established him as the undisputed leader. He was called the "king of Shirataki."

In 1915 Morihei met the man who would influence his budo more than any other: Sokaku Takeda, master of the Daito style of jujutsu, which was said to have been passed down in the Takeda family from the imperial lineage of Seiwa-genji (1021 c.e.). Takeda was a small man, a few inches shorter even than Ueshiba. Until he met Takeda-sensei, Morihei had never been defeated by anyone. Although Morihei was by far the stronger of the two, he was nevertheless thrown every time by Takeda's superior technique. When asked later if he had learned the secret of aikido from Takeda's Daito jujutsu, Morihei replied, "No, aikido came later. Takeda-sensei opened my eyes to the principle of budo." From the earliest times, the imperial household had kept the teachings of budo and the universal principle underlying it as well-guarded secrets. With the coming of the feudal period and the rise of the samurai class in the early 1200s, this budo became more widely available and some great budo masters arose. Takeda was descended from this lineage.

In January 1919 Morihei received word that his father was very ill. He left Hokkaido immediately and started home. En route, he heard rumors of a spiritual master named Wanisaburo Deguchi in Ayabe. As this was on his way, he decided to stop there to pray for his father. He also hoped that he might be able to meet Deguchi.

Wanisaburo Deguchi, a famous figure in Japanese history, was a spiritual leader of a quality unparalleled in modern times. Because his teachings differed radically from those of traditional Shinto, he was also known as one of the three most wanted "bandits" in Japan. He was often forced to retreat into the mountains to continue his spiritual training—treks on which, later, Ueshiba would accompany him, both as a bodyguard and for his own spiritual training.

Deguchi founded a new sect of Shinto that reputedly revived long-lost original teachings. He wrote hundreds of books concerning the spiritual world and the teachings of his sect, O-moto Kyo (the great origin). He had a tremendous influence on the religious and philo-sophical climate of his country. When he died, the mourners following his coffin numbered in the thousands. It was through his relationship with Wanisaburo Deguchi that Morihei came to study the kototama and the ancient teachings of Shinto in depth.

Stepping off the train platform at Ayabe station, Morihei was amazed at the number of people around him. Many of them were dressed in traditional kimono or ceremonial costume. Following the crowd, he came to stand in front of two beautiful, large golden temples. Entering one, he proceeded to the sanctuary and knelt to pray. When he opened his eyes again, a man in white robes stood over him. "Did you see anything?" the man asked. "Yes," replied Morihei, "I saw the ailing face of my father." "It's all right for him," answered Deguchi. Morihei considered the meaning of Deguchi's words: his father was dying of natural causes and there was no need to be anxious about him because there was nothing he could do. The bond that formed between Ueshiba and Deguchi was one of mutual admiration and respect and lasted until Deguchi's death in 1948.

When Morihei arrived home, his father had already passed away. Yoroku's final words for his son were, "Live your life freely and accom-plish whatever you wish." These were difficult words for Morihei to accept. His father had always done everything for him; now he wanted to do something in return.

After his father's death, Morihei changed drastically. He became as one possessed, going off into the mountains where he was seen swing-ing his sword at phantoms in the air. Rumors began circulating that a dangerous, crazy man was living in the mountains, and soldiers were recruited to fetch him out. They were amazed when they discovered

■ *Wanisaburo Deguchi*

Morihei, the man who had been their honored army superior and teacher of sword skills. Falling to their knees, they bowed and asked him to return with them to the village. Morihei, after a stressful three months, complied and returned to Tanabe. Once there, however, he told his relatives that he had decided not to stay, bid them farewell and returned to Ayabe to join the O-moto Kyo of Wanisaburo Deguchi.

"I'm glad to see you. I anticipated you would come!" Deguchi said upon Morihei's arrival. "There is, however, no need for you to work for O-moto Kyo. Your mission is to develop a new martial art which will aid mankind!" Deguchi was the first to recognize Morihei's potential both as a spiritual leader as well as a martial artist. So Ueshiba, now thirty-five, began his studies of Shinto with the O-moto sect. From the spiritual vision gained from these studies came the unique constitution of aikido, a martial art based on the kototama, the true substance of universal law.

With Deguchi's help, Morihei started a dojo near the O-moto head-quarters, calling his style *aiki bujutsu*. At this dojo the form of aikido began to take shape. Through his studies of Shinto, Morihei found the missing aspect of spirituality that would set aikido apart from other martial forms. He came to see aikido as the embodiment of a living prayer for world health, harmony, and prosperity.

Morihei's spiritual understanding elevated his martial ability to a level incomprehensible to other martial artists of his time. His ability has not been duplicated even to this day. He would throw his students one at a time or as they attacked in a group, and without visibly touching them. The students claimed they felt nothing, but were sent flying through the air.

In his verbal teachings, Morihei expounded on universal laws and scientific principles that are only in recent times becoming the object of scientific investigation. His explanations were couched in the symbolic terms of Shinto mythology. He declared, "These are not my teachings but the teachings of the imperial lineage of Japan. Nevertheless, the actual training in these principles is the practice of aikido."

Both men and women entered his dojo and he accepted students from all over Japan. Many martial arts masters came to test the growing reputation of Ueshiba-sensei. He defeated them one by one—and sometimes in groups, taking on several at a time. Sometimes he would do simple things like hold out a piece of paper and ask someone to try to grasp it. No one could even touch it. Masters of other martial arts were among of his first students. They said that his mysterious ability was reminiscent of the prowess of masters of ages past.

"Using the extremely difficult language of ancient Shinto, it is hardly possible to explain things in an understandable way to our modern age," said D.T. Suzuki, one of the earliest proponents of Zen Buddhism in the West. "Nevertheless, the teaching and practice of Morihei Ueshiba is at one with that of Mahayana Buddhism, and also the way of Zen. They will be future proof of each other. Although it is not based on any formal study of Zen Buddhism, Ueshiba-sensei's experience is definitely what is referred to in the Far East as *satori*. The words of this great teacher should be recorded for the future. Through them an understanding of a new kind of intelligence might someday be reached."[3]

A college professor and long-time student of Zen Buddhism corroborated Suzuki-sensei's appraisal: "Until I began to study aikido, there was always something about Zen that I couldn't grasp at all. Aikido is Zen in motion and it brings the reality of Zen to the surface."

In his book *Ken to Zen* (Zen and Japanese swordsmanship), Sogen Omori, a master swordsman of the Choku Shin Kage style, recalled his experience of meeting Ueshiba-sensei: "I was attending a certain gathering and noticed an elderly gentleman sitting formally on his knees. After studying him for a few minutes I was amazed to discover that I could find no place of weakness, no opening *[suki]* where he might be attacked. He was sitting calmly, watching the events around him, yet his mind was absolutely clear and in a state of constant readiness. I concluded that this must be the famous Ueshiba-sensei, and I was introduced to him as such a moment later."

Although he had a deep respect for the depth and value of true Zen, Ueshiba-sensei disliked the self-styled Zen of modern times and refused to discuss Zen philosophy or satori. He stated that aikido itself was the way through which all theory and conceptualism is left behind and self-realization gained:

> *Aikido is not born from religion. The real takemusubi aiki shines*
> *forth like a powerful beacon light and illuminates religion. It leads*
> *to fullness those partial, imperfect, and temporary teachings of the*
> *past. Among most religious leaders of today there is no method for*

the accomplishment or realization of their ideals. There is no way for them to weigh their own understanding.

We cannot put our lives in the hands of Christ, the Buddha, or the teachings of Confucius. The age of prophecy [philosophy] is finished. We are now living in the time of actual training. Each and every person must become the god of the center [Ame no Mi Naka Nushi]. This is the reality of the empty sky, the total existence. We are not merely the divided spirit of one God. All the gods of the universe are our protective spirits.

Although Ueshiba-sensei never studied Zen formally, he was definitely influenced by its teachings. Among the styles of Japanese sword that he studied, the one most strongly influenced by Zen was Yagyu Ryu. To explain the mental stance of aikido, Ueshiba-sensei often quoted the teachings of Takuan-zenji (1573–1645), the spiritual teacher of Yagyu Munenori. Takuan is perhaps best known for shaping the destiny of Japan's most famous swordsman, Miyamoto Musashi (1584–1645). Musashi was undefeated in over sixty matches before the age of twenty-nine, and the last half of his life was devoted to Zen study, meditation, and art.

The influence of Japanese swordsmanship on aikido is one of the main factors separating aikido from jujutsu. Aikido does not throw, as happens in judo or jujutsu. Aikido cuts, without a sword. *Zen* and *sword* are inseparable in Japanese history. Both had a tremendous influence on the development of aikido.

Takuan's "immoveable wisdom" (*fudochi shinmyo ryoku*) makes this point clear. "Where shall we place our mind? If we concentrate on our partner's movement, our mind will be captured by it. If we concentrate on his sword, our mind will be captured by his sword. If we concentrate on the place we wish to cut, the result is the same. Concentrating on escaping his blade, the result is still the same. In a word, there is no place to put our mind."[4] O-sensei also subscribed to this teaching, adding:

You must not look at your partner at all. Rather you should train yourself to absorb his mind and ki. When he strikes with shomen [a direct overhead strike] my sword point will already be resting at his throat or I will be cutting him from behind.

Takuan used the example of Senshu no Kannon, the goddess of mercy with one thousand arms, to express ultimate freedom and nonattachment. "The body must move with complete freedom and the mind without attachment to that movement." This is also the ideal of aikido. It is described in the Zen expression *mujushin*: the mind of no abode or stopping place. It contains both *fudoshin* (imperturbable mind) and *zanshin* (unbroken concentration), terms used in the teaching of aikido.

In aikido, *mujushin* is to move with whole body and mind, at one with both movement and rest. It is to move with complete stability and centeredness, in harmony with our partner and unattached to the success of our technique. This mind is a goal of both Zen and aikido. Its awesome power and gentility are represented in the Great Buddha (Dai-butsu) statue at Kamakura, Japan (see figure 1.1).

O-sensei prescribed three stages of training for his students. The first puts the mind in order; that is, in harmony with universal function. This makes the mind the dutiful servant of the will so that it is no longer moved by the senses or the whims of the ego. This is *Masakatsu*, the

■ *Figure 1.1: Dai-butsu. Photo by Larry Lieberman.*

clear judgment and direct perception which makes spontaneous movement possible. It is the correct intention, the foundation of all spiritual training.

The second stage harmonizes the body, our entire being, with that same universal order. This body-mind unification or *Shin Shin Toitsu* is the beginning of self mastery, *Agatsu*. The final stage puts the ki that unifies mind and body into harmony with universal order. In this stage one loses all sense of knowing anything: all skillfulness is gone. There is no difference between oneself and anyone else. This O-sensei referred to as *katsu hayabi*.

O-sensei taught,

> *One's real body is the universe itself, and one's responsibility as a human being encompasses all things therein.*

This does not mean to know God—which is an impossibility—but rather to eliminate the separation between self and other. There is no ego remaining to make meaningless distinctions between oneself and others. This is not a one-time experience of awakening but a constant awareness resulting from years of experience and training. This is not a matter of pietism, and it contains no sense of greatness or lack of greatness. It is an intimate communion in which nature verifies one's existence.

Ueshiba-sensei's first experience of satori occurred in the spring of 1925, when he was forty-one years old. During a visit by an old army friend, there was a disagreement. His old comrade grabbed a wooden sword *(bokken)* and attempted to hit him. He kept trying until he became exhausted, finally giving up and leaving in anger. Ueshiba-sensei was left standing alone in his garden.

> *All of a sudden I felt like the sky was descending. From out of the earth, golden energy was spouting forth like a fountain. That warm energy encircled me and my body and mind became very light and clear. I could even understand the murmurings of the small birds around me. At that moment I could understand that my life's work in budo was actually based on divine love and the laws of creation. I was unable to stop my tears and I wept freely. Since that time I've known that this great earth itself is my house and home. The sun,*

moon, and stars each belong to me. Since that time I've never felt
any attachment to property or possessions.

This experience resembles that of Jesus of Nazareth after his forty days of fasting and prayer, or that of Moses as he gazed into the burning bush on the sacred mountain. Essentially, it is the merging of an individual will with that of universal spirit. The individual being is so closely united with the spirit of creation that every thought and feeling is like an echo, an immediate response to the will of God. Buddha called out to Ananda, his closest student, "Ananda!" Immediately the answer, "Yes, master!" The Buddha was then silent and the teaching was complete. This event is often said to be like the pecking and tapping that goes on between the chick in the egg and the mother hen on the outside. If they don't communicate perfectly the chick will either suffocate or be hatched prematurely. O-sensei stated,

When you bow to the universe, it bows back; when you call out
the name of God, it echoes inside you.

Aikido is a method of merging with the kototama, the spirit of the universe. As such it is *inori*, a moving form of prayer. Although prayer today is thought of as a method of asking for divine favor, originally it was a method of blending our own ki with the kototama and universal order. In the words of O-sensei,

According to the ancient writings of Shinto, the word takemusu
means the most unique essence of budo, the principle by which
one realizes his true nature as a god and finds ultimate freedom.
From this principle, unlimited technique is born from divine power.

In some cases, this merging is accompanied by hearing "the voice of God." The Christian may interpret it as the voice of Jesus Christ; the Buddhist may say that it is the voice of Kannon, the goddess of mercy. This voice is heard when we merge with our infinite nature, the life will itself. The esoteric practices of Shinto aim at this merging of individual spirit with that of the universe. It is thus not surprising that Ueshiba-sensei, who practiced Shinto purification rites with extreme intensity, should have this kind of experience:

It was on December 14, which strangely enough coincides with my birthday. After practicing suigyo [chanting under a waterfall] for about an hour, I began to experience something extraordinary. I felt the presence of my guardian spirit, Sarutahiko Ohkami, descend upon me. . . . Then I heard a voice saying "I am the guardian diety of aikido,[5] which creates all things through the function of infinite oneness. I have entered into the very essence of your being. Now is the time for you to stand up and purify the world."

I fought with the reality of this experience and although I became quite ill, I continued my military obligations and the teaching of young soldiers. One evening I was in my garden practicing sword. Suddenly a ghostlike duplicate of myself appeared before me. I tried to strike the figure but its sword immediately penetrated my defense. I wasn't allowed the slightest margin for carelessness or error.

At first my movement was too slow but gradually it improved. When I was able to cut my opponent's bokken down, he vanished. This training continued for two weeks. Sometimes I lost the feeling of holding the bokken at all and my physical body only remained as the breath of the universe within my hara. I realized that the deepest enlightenment of budo is one with that of religion and tears of ecstacy flowed freely.

O-sensei's extrasensory ability continued to increase. He could sense people's intentions, even at considerable distances, and he was impossible to deceive. He invited his students to attack him at any time. They made attempts when he was about to put food in his mouth, or when he was in the bathroom, but he always anticipated their intentions before they could attack. He had a habit of looking directly at them just as they were about to attack and he would look up at them as he lifted his chopsticks. He was allegedly challenged by a man who taunted him with, "Aikido cannot defeat a gun." He accepted the challenge. When the man raised the gun he was already standing behind him. When asked how it was done he replied only, "You can't do that often, it takes years off your life."

Ueshiba-sensei's life bore witness to his lack of attachment. He spent his last funds, "God's money," for improvements to the dojo. Once he received a large sum of money for an aikido demonstration in an envelope labeled *Tip*. Angrily he returned the money saying, "I don't accept tips." The envelope was relabeled *In gratitude*, and one of the students carefully and with an ounce of humor gave it to him again. This time he accepted it, but returned it to the students for their personal needs.

Once an applicant visited the dojo and made the mistake of asking how much aikido classes cost. "Fool, do you think that the understanding of aikido can be bought at any price!" roared Morihei. At fifty years of age he still had a voice like a young lion. Not uncommonly, students were shaken by a sudden shout, only to find O-sensei laughing jovially in the next moment, as if nothing had happened.

Here is an episode taken from George Ohsawa's *The Art of Peace*:

> The famous boxing champion Horiguchi, "The Piston," came one day to the master's dojo and requested a match. The master invited him to attack with all his power and ability. The boxer attacked violently by crashing continuous blows to the chest of the master, who suddenly countered by striking both of the boxer's arms from the outside with his two hands. It was a single, flexible, almost invisible strike. Horiguchi fell to the ground with two broken arms and spent two months in the hospital.

O-sensei explained it in this way:

> *Aikido is the way of nonresistance and is therefore undefeatable from the start. Fast and slow are of no consequence. Merely by having the intention to fight with one who embodies the universal law, they have fixed their mind on violating the harmony of nature itself. The person with evil or malicious feeling [jyaki] is defeated before he makes the first move. The contest has already been decided.*
>
> *This being so, in what way can we rid ourselves of this* jyaki *and become pure of spirit and mind? We must unify our mind and feeling with the mercy and compassion of the universal spirit. Within love [ai], there is no competition, no enemy, no antagonism toward anyone else or anything. Those whose feeling does not coincide with this mentality can in no way come into harmony with the laws of the universe.*

In 1927 O-sensei left the O-moto sect and moved again to Tokyo, where he continued to teach and open new dojos. His students became so numerous that he constantly needed a new and larger space. Eventually he required all new students to have at least two recommendations to enter the dojo. In l930, with the help of many supporters, he enlarged a smaller facility in the Wakamatsu district of Shinjuku, Tokyo, to a mat-space of over fourteen hundred square feet. It was called Kobukan Dojo (the present world headquarters, Honbu Dojo).

The practice at Kobukan Dojo was so intense that the dojo came to be known as the Hell Dojo of Wakamatsu Cho. O-sensei felt, however, that aikido must be understood as a spiritual discipline and not merely as a method of fighting. He was deeply troubled by the inability of world cooperation and the intensifying war effort. In his words:

> Aikido is the function of universal harmony expressed through the human body.

In 1942 O-sensei moved to Iwama prefecture and returned to farming, contemplation, and prayer. In spite of his great ability he chose to live in poverty and train himself constantly. He made a special request to the head priest of the ancient Tsubaki shrine and had the deity Sarutahiko Ohkami enshrined in the Aiki shrine. Sarutahiko Ohkami, who O-sensei considered as his guardian spirit, is the pioneer of righteousness and justice and the head of all the earthly deities (Amaterasu Oh Mi Kami is the head of all the heavenly deities).

At the end of World War II a ban on all teachings of martial arts was imposed on Japan by the occupation government. In 1948, when this ban was lifted, aikido again began to become active in society. Its organizational name was changed from Kobukan to the Aikikai Foundation, and Kisshomaru Ueshiba, the founder's son, became *doshu*, the head of the dojo. Since then, the fame and influence of aikido has continued to spread and increase throughout the world.

The content of aikido was expressed through every aspect of O-sensei's life. He held that the value of a pure, truthful, and sincere heart was equivalent to godliness. He was firm in his understanding that the power of aikido, as well as any seemingly individual power, is not the possession of an individual, but that we are always the receivers *(ukemi)* of the gift, from beginning to end. His poetry expresses this attitude:

> *Touched by the true heart* [makoto],
> *train and deepen your understanding therein.*
> *Resolved in the oneness of this world*
> *and the world to follow.*
>
> *Aikido, all power brought into motion creating*
> *a world of beauty, gentility, and tranquillity.*
>
> *Entrusting all to the flow of divine heavenly*
> *consciousness, the breath of heaven and earth;*
> *the true man, fully utilizing the mind of God.*
>
> *Standing in this mountain stream, I wonder why it*
> *is that no man can speak as truthfully as the sound*
> *of the water against the rock.*[6]

The rock is the steadfast will. In Japanese, the same kototama, *ishi*, is used for both *will* and *rock*. By the virtue of heaven's centripetalism (universal will), the rock (human will) is rooted firmly to the earth. This is not willfulness but self-mastery.

The horizontal waves of the mountain stream constantly hit against the rock. They are the vicissitudes of life. The sound of the water against the rock is the birth of new consciousness, new kototama. The entire scene exemplifies fudoshin, immovable mind: relaxed, at peace, it is completely stable. Within movement there is "something" that does not move. It may be said to be the source of change itself.

When he was seventy, Ueshiba-sensei's aikido reached the height of its beauty. His public demonstrations were a thing of beauty and wonder for all who saw them. He would chant Oom Oomuu, saying, "the dance of the gods begins." Dressed in white kimono and moving with lightning speed and power, he truly appeared to be a god. At the age of seventy-seven he was honored by the Japanese emperor for his work. Continuing to practice until his last days, he would be helped from behind as he climbed the stairs to the third-floor dojo. When he stepped onto the mat, however, he was transformed and no one could even touch him.

■ *Kagura mai: The dance of the gods*

On April 26, 1969, Morihei Ueshiba passed away, leaving to his students his dream of the world as one peaceful family through the practice of aikido. On that same day, the Japanese government conferred upon him the Order of the Sacred Treasure, the most highly esteemed of the many honors he received for the creation of aikido.

Aikido students still gather at the Aiki shrine each year to honor Ueshiba-sensei and his teachings. His message remains as an inspiration to all aikidoka.

> *Aikido must elucidate the order of the universe and the path toward spiritual understanding. We have the responsibility for the well-being of this planet and all life upon it. Failing to meet this responsibility, we can never realize our true nature or become happy and free. When we grasp our actual substance, life becomes devoted to the realization of the dreams of our ancestors since ancient times. That is to establish the paradise on earth: to create the mirror image of the heavenly world on this earth. Our individual practice of aikido is a barometer of this activity.*
>
> *Budo is not a matter of physical strength, the handling of weapons with great skill, nor the ability to strike another person down before he can do the same thing to you. It is the path toward eternal wisdom and spiritual understanding. Nevertheless, if it is not effective in actual practice, it loses its spiritual value and uniqueness as well. In the true budo, there is no enemy. You shouldn't train to become strong or to be able to defeat an enemy but rather that you can be of use to world peace.*

2 ▪ THE WAY OF HARMONY

AIKIDO IS MOST COMMONLY TRANSLATED AS "the way of harmony." *Do* is the Tao, the way; *ki* translates as "spiritual energy"; and the most all-encompassing meaning of *ai* is "harmony." Harmony is blending with our environment by changing difficulties into joy and conflict into peace. This need not be merely a lofty concept. It can become a practical reality through the development of real power. To the degree that this is accomplished, *ai* also takes on the meaning of "love" or "compassion."

▪ *Aikido*

▪ *Love*   ▪ *Harmony*

Ueshiba Morihei taught that love and harmony are synonymous and implicit in the meaning of aikido. The harmony of nature is the source of unlimited power, the source of all our energy and abilities. There is no love without power, only the need for fulfillment. The purpose of aikido training is to bring forth our true nature, to develop the spiritual power which is our innate heritage.

What is aikido? This is not a question to be answered simply. Attempts to explain aikido through technique or philosophy alone are caught up in dualism. Aikido is an intuitive study of human life. Aikido contains the foundation of the ancient martial arts, yet it is also the fruition or blossoming of those ancient practices. Its beautiful and powerful techniques are ideal martial forms. Aikido has been labeled "wrist-twisting," "receiving conflict without opposition," and "using your partner's strength against him." Such descriptions contain degrees of validity, yet none of them grasps aikido's spiritual content.

Martial arts in general can be divided into three categories. The first category concentrates on striking the enemy; the second attempts to control him; and the third, most difficult, attempts to upset his balance and throw him down. Aikido contains all of these, yet expresses them through its own unique principle.

Throwing in aikido is different from judo. In aikido you unify with your partner's intention and redirect his or her force to lead your partner off balance. Controlling is also different from other martial arts techniques such as shaolin kung fu *(chin na)* or jujutsu. Rather than controlling through pain or injury to the joints, aikido concentrates the mind in such a way that your partner receives the intensity of your power throughout his body (especially at his center of balance) more than at the place of contact. This reduces the possibility of a counter-attack, as he is unable to discover the source of the power controlling him. The main emphasis of aikido training should be on control.

Striking *(atemi)* in aikido has great potential power: it can cause serious injury to the internal organs. The founder taught that one blow could kill a man but that the use of this unrestrained power is unnecessary and unacceptable for practice. Atemi should be used to lead your partner's mind rather than to injure him.

Aikido is usually practiced as a hand-to-hand form, yet its essence derives from the art of Japanese swordsmanship. The highest teaching *(okugi)* of sword, called *aiki*, refers to a method of escaping unharmed without cutting your partner. It is also called *ai nuki*. In the Yagyu style of sword it is *katsu jin ken*, the sword that gives life (*satsu jin ken* is the sword that kills).

In aikido, as in swordsmanship, any attempt to control your partner through physical force makes you vulnerable. To see the reality of any situation, you must see it not only with your physical eyes but also with your mind's eye, the eye of intuition. To be successful, your body and mind must be alert and free from tension. In aikido speed or physical power is much less important than the development of an all-embracing attitude. This is not apparent to the inexperienced observer; indeed, it is understood by the aspiring aikidoka only after years of training. Despite its formality, aikido is not static. It is decided in the moment, before technique even appears.

Movement begins in the center of the *hara,* the *tanden no ichi* or "one point," where the aikidoka's mind is focused. The spiritual content of aikido can be expressed in the one word *hara,* which ranges in meaning from "belly" to "heart-mind" or "soul." Hara is not only the physical center of the body; properly understood, it is also the center of our spiritual energy. The kototama of hara is *ha* (eight) and *ra* (spiraling outward). Much the same as the heart pumps out blood to nourish the physical cells of the body, hara distributes ki to all parts of the body. This process of ki distribution can be controlled by concentration. In the center of the brain is another energy-producing center, or hara, from which new consciousness (word souls) is born. When these two centers are combined, great spiritual power can be realized.

Kototama is a many-faceted Japanese concept for which there is no equivalent in English. Kototama is one and many: it can be described as the invisible world of spirit, the divine plan, and the creative energy of life. It is the dimensions of ki that give structure to the forms of the material universe. These dimensions will be explored further in chapters 4, 5, and 6.

Practicing aikido day in and day out, these two hara centers become united vertically; the will becomes rooted in the body's physical center and the excess activity of the mind ceases. Heaven (mind) and earth (body) are united through spirit (the will). In this way the total meaning of hara, body-mind, is realized. We come to embody the Japanese expressions, *hara de kangaeru,* to think with one's hara, and *hara de yaru,* to act from hara.

This process of developing hara in aikido shares common points with the development of *samadhi* in Zen. In each, the practitioner must penetrate beyond dualistic thought to the basis of *heijoshin,* or everyday mind. In the case of Zen, "The initial aim of sitting zen (zazen) is samadhi, the condition of total stillness, in which body and mind are fallen off, no thought stirs, the mind is empty, yet we are in a state of extreme wakefulness. This is the state known as absolute samadhi or pure existence. In this state, kensho (satori) is latent. Working samadhi is a state where the normal activity of consciousness is arrested yet the mind is still active with

■ *Hara*

what it is concentrating on."[1] Aikido helps to remind us of our natural state of being. It is a kind of working samadhi within which intuitive research continues to function. The spiritual power of hara is to manifest technique spontaneously while moving in complete harmony with one's partner. This requires great faith or trust in one's self.

For example, if someone attempts to restrain your freedom of movement and you allow your mind to be drawn into that conflict, you have already lost yourself. By allowing your mind to be drawn out from your center, you have lost control and the opportunity to deal with conflict reasonably. You must be able to cut through your partner's intention with the sword of judgment. The moment your opponent moves, your mind must already have him under control. By attempting to immobilize you, he—or she—becomes caught in the net of your ki. Through attachment to his purpose, the opponent is locked like a magnet and must conform to your movement.

Aikido is often said to be the art of using an opponent's energy against himself. It is not, however, a matter of action and reaction, skillfulness, or technique. It is a system of self-defense, yet, unlike other martial forms, it is not a method of destruction. Aikido is the art of becoming of one mind and body with the opponent. This requires being firmly centered and aware of one's own existence. One's will must be concentrated in the hara. Practiced properly, aikido enables the practitioner to bring mind and body under the control of the will. This leads to both wisdom and control—the ability to transform difficulties and aggression into joy and self-improvement. Based on universal order, aikido creates health in both body and spirit.

MAKOTO

The highest virtue of the warrior is *makoto*, or simply, *ma*: to be true to oneself and to others. This is the origin of *aiki*. It requires living in the moment, beyond conceptuality or self-seeking motivation. It is sincerity and honesty; seeing things just as they are. This kind of sincerity results from selflessness, the intimacy that eliminates duality. Ueshiba-sensei expressed it as *katsu hayabi*—instantaneous attainment— immersed in the moment beyond space and time. This is *ma-ai*, the

■ *Makoto*

perfect interval between self and partner, which renders both speed and timing insignificant.

Aikido training leads us toward both health and judgment, yet unless we deliberately direct ourselves toward makoto, sincerity and reality, our progress will be slow and self-realization lacking. The spiritual content of aikido is not to be found in any fixed form or technique. It is our own consciousness that gives spiritual power to aikido form. Lacking correct mentality and intention, we can only discover the physical aspects of aikido—there will be little progress beyond fourth or fifth dan. This is true of all spiritual disciplines. Our progress is roughly equivalent to the amount of effort put forth, yet until we abandon our ego and let nature's power flow through us, even effort is not enough.

Of course, we can also lose the way by becoming too serious. In the words of Erasmus, "To play the fool in season is the height of wisdom." To be overly concerned about progress is attachment.

There is the story of a young swordsman wishing to study with the master Banzo. He approached the master saying, "My father is old and I have to return home soon to care for him, how long will it take me to master the sword?" "Ten years," said Banzo. Taken aback, the man rephrased his question. "Please understand me. I am willing to work day and night. How long will it take me then?" "Thirty years!" replied Banzo. "A student in such a hurry makes very slow progress."

If we are to grasp aikido's principle, we must practice very hard yet maintain a flexible attitude. We must combine both seriousness and adaptability. We must learn to excel in nondoing, and this requires an attitude of fierce determination.

The importance of attitude has been emphasized in the martial arts since ancient times. Japanese swordsmanship cites the ten evils or mistaken states of mind: excessive pride (putting up with too much), anger, overconfidence, meekness, hatred, greed (insatiability), fear, contempt, doubt, and illusion (superstition). In short, we should have no confidence and no lack of confidence.

Another story tells of a man who took a fighting cock to a trainer to be prepared for competition. The man returned a week later and asked if the bird was ready. The trainer replied, "No, when he hears another cock in the distance he still ruffles up his feathers." Somewhat confused the cock's owner left, returning a few days later. "Is the bird ready for combat?" he asked. "Yes," the trainer replied, "even when another bird approaches he shows no reaction at all!" Until we are free of both fear and aggression, we cannot master aikido feeling or technique.

Aikido is *michi*, a way of life: its practice aligns body, mind, and spirit with the creative energy, or ki, of nature. O-sensei referred to this energy as One Spirit, Four Souls, Three Origins, and Eight Powers: the content and function of universal law. It is further divided into fifty different vibrations that, when spoken or even thought of, influence us physically, mentally, and spiritually. Aikido allows us intimately to experience our natural state of being by conforming to the divine plan of universal order (kototama) as expressed through the human body.

Aikido enables us to experience the spiritual content of apparent reality. In order to grasp this, however, we must be free of presuppositions. Beginner's mind and faith based on experience are essential if we are to experience the creative impetus of life as our own inherent nature. True aikido begins from this inner sense. Technique is only the beginning of training. We use technique to train in the principles of natural movement, yet it is our spiritual substance, our true self, that dictates spontaneity.

The study of technique and form helps us to discover the underlying feeling of aikido. When we get acquainted with this feeling, correct technique occurs automatically. This is the interdependent study of body and spirit. The poet Walt Whitman stated, "I see a man building a house that will serve him a few years . . . or seventy or eighty years at most; I see one building the house that serves him longer than that!"[2] The first man is taking care of the body; the second, the spirit. Aikido training builds both body and spirit. This is the goal of many religious and aesthetic disciplines, yet few have the means to accomplish and verify that goal. This is where aikido stands out.

Steeped in the truths underlying religion, philosophy, and natural law, aikido, for many practitioners, elucidates these teachings. Bridging and encompassing them, it brings them to life with a renewed sense of validity. To become one with this wisdom is different from studying it conceptually. Spiritual understanding that cannot be expressed as ability remains just that: an idea. In the words of the late Tibetan Buddhist teacher Chögyam Trungpa-rinpoche, "There is a natural order and harmony in this world which we can discover. But we can't just study that order scientifically or measure it mathematically. We have to feel it in our bones, in our hearts, in our minds."[3]

Aikido is the study of ourselves as individuals and also as members of society. It teaches us the interdependency of all things and makes us aware of our common purpose as human beings. We learn to defeat our egocentricity and discover the futility of competing with others. Aikido teaches us how to resolve the contradictions of daily life.

When we are grasped by difficulty, we imagine that we are limited to the confines of the physical body, the shoulders tighten and we react defensively. We lose our innate freedom and become trapped in a self-created illusion. If, however, we are unhindered by the illusion of separation, our real substance responds. Then we experience freedom of movement and spontaneous creativity. Aikido practice is the practice of this freedom.

The conventional modern mind stresses the concept that more is better. Large muscles are equated with health and power, a large bankroll with happiness and success, a huge arsenal with national security. Like ostriches sticking their heads in the sand, we create walls of ego or self-esteem to hide behind. We fortify the barriers further by becoming aggressive and unreasonable. When the walls are taken away, we see them to be made of empty and self-created illusions. Depression and mental illness are also fears created by the illusion of separation. Just as a child separated from its mother may be overcome with fear and unable to care for its own needs, when we perceive ourselves to be separate from our spiritual parents (heaven—the life-will; and earth—instinct, nature), we become unable to cope with our lives.

How have we grown so estranged from our nature? Why have we become spiritual orphans living in fear? We have lost both physiological and ideological orientation. Our physical orientation depends mainly on our connection with nature and the earth—in other words, on our daily diet. Improper diet leads to a severance of our instinct-intuition faculty, our spiritual lifeline, our hara. We turn from experience, or intuitive understanding, to *thinking*—living in our heads—adrift on the stormy ocean of uncontrolled mind without a compass (judgment) or stabilizing anchor (will). As Fritjof Capra stated: "Descartes' famous sentence [*cogito ergo sum*—I think, therefore I am] expresses the Western identification of self with mind, instead of with existence itself. In keeping with the Cartesian division, most individuals are aware of themselves as isolated egos existing [inside] their bodies."[4]

The illusion of separation must be replaced by spiritual fortitude, the faith and confidence that result from actual training. Our true, heaven-given substance, the life-will, created both mind and body. Constantly, it preserves this creation as its own child. When we once again become intimate with our selves, attachment and fear disappear. This reorientation can be accomplished through the practice of aikido.

Correct technique in aikido requires an intimate communication between yourself and your partner. Always treat your partner with respect and consideration. To injure another student is unskillful: it shows a lack of judgment and control. There should be no thought of defending yourself. The mind of defense is the same violent, fighting mind as that of offense. In aikido, both offense and defense disappear in the process of conflict resolution.

Developing an attitude of responsibility for the well-being of others leads not only to the aikidoka's progress but also to the improvement of society. Just as the motions and internal functions of the body are expressions of mind and spirit, so the quality of society is the collective expression of the human race. The process of creation lies not only within each individual but also within humanity's collective consciousness. Social change begins with responsible individuals of high judgment and moral character; it is not the result of intellectual study or virtuous teachings, but the product of sensitivity and judgment based on experience and spiritual training.

The spirit of aikido is a parental feeling for all people. This intimate feeling does not judge or make separation between self and other. Modern interpretations of morality and justice, however, tend to be rigid and rule-bound. Lacking flexibility, they often become the source of violence.

The Eastern idea of morality begins with the idea of innate human virtue, an idea that is flexible and able to adapt to changing situations. The Buddhist Kukai, for one, taught that morality consists of mastering the teachings, never giving up the aspiration for enlightenment, sharing the teachings with others, and benefiting others.[5] Fritjof Capra has observed, "In the East a virtuous person is not one who undertakes the impossible task of striving for the good and eliminating the bad but rather one who is able to maintain a dynamic balance between good and bad."[6] Lao-tzu expressed it thus, "When all the world recognizes the good as the good, this is only the bad."[7] In Japan, the single most important factor of morality is summed up in the word *omoiyari*: mutual consideration for the feelings of others.

True morality is the warrior spirit itself; to live and die for justice and the improvement of human society. O-sensei remarked, "Aikido is undefeatable because it doesn't fight." There are many statements that reflect the true spirit of the warrior. Jesus of Nazareth taught, "Resist no evil: but whosoever shall smite thee on thy right cheek, turn to him the other also."[8] And Will Rogers stated, "I never met a man I didn't like." These statements speak of a spirit of flexibility that is combined with selflessness and determination.

The person who seeks conflict with others is a coward, afraid to confront the real enemy within. In the samurai tradition, drawing one's sword unnecessarily was seen as cowardice and poor judgment. The virtue of the warrior lies not in defeating others but in standing on the earth, completely aware of one's own existence. Such a mentality—unconcerned with competition or appearing good in the eyes of others—is our inherent nature, sometimes hidden but never lost.

In aikido, the warrior spirit is expressed firstly as makoto: to be true to oneself and also to others; secondly, as beginner's mind: endlessly to seek further perfection; and thirdly, as a dedication to relieve the suffering of all people. By teaching surrender of the sense of competition and the desire to defeat others, aikido provides the tools for developing these virtues and paves the road toward still deeper changes.

Through the physical practice of aikido, we experience ourselves as spiritual beings. All of one's existence becomes an expression of hara—body, mind, and spirit as one. One learns to manifest spiritual energy to unite with the external environment. This experience transforms the way one sees and deals with life. We learn the value of blending with, rather than opposing, difficulties. In a word, we become *sunao*.

SUNAO

The character of one who has realized makoto is *sunao*. To be sunao is to combine flexibility and power in one's character and adjust one's feeling to the kototama of *Su,* the ki of nonresistance. It is a state of neither knowing nor not knowing; neither confident nor insecure. It occurs as a natural result of training. The kototama of Su brings our senses into peaceful unity; our life becomes fresh and spontaneous. With the feeling of separation and excessive desire eliminated, clear

▪ *Sunao*

vision becomes possible. The quality of one who is sunao is like a flower in the desert: in its presence, all who see it feel happy. We become *mikoto*, the mirror image of makoto manifest here and now.

Through daily training in aikido, we begin to incorporate the conflict-resolving power of nonresistance and nondoing. This is harmonizing our feelings and actions with the kototama of *su*. Each of us must discover this power within ourselves, yet regardless of genius or natural talent, it cannot be grasped through effort alone.

I remember attending an evening class in which I was having a particularly difficult time. In the middle of practicing a technique, I became unable to move and heard my teacher shout, "*Yaroo to omotte iru da kara* (It's because you think that *you* are going to *do* it)." Aikido technique can never be correct as long as an individual *does* it! It is a matter of correct *being*—being that allows things to happen naturally. Whatever we are able to accomplish, it is not merely by our own power.

To paraphrase a lecture given by the aikido shihan Kazuo Chiba,

> Anyone who thinks that merely putting in many hours of training will necessarily result in great achievement is thinking like a child. This leads to an unsolvable problem. Progress in aikido moves in proportion to the discovery of a natural power, an organic, dynamic core within oneself. This helps the body to function in harmony, as a whole.
>
> Aikido is a path where one progressively encounters the true self with wonder and joy; the estranged self, hidden with its inexhaustable potential, lies undiscovered by many people who die without even knowing that it exists. Our body is a product of our consciousness, and discovering what that product is requires close self-examination. It is not a path where one adds more and more information, details, power, etc., externally and endlessly, to the too much that is already there.

Ueshiba-sensei trained in many unreasonable ways. After his enlightenment and the subsequent creation of aikido, he claimed:

> *I created aikido so that others wouldn't have to endure such foolish training. Why do you persist in meaningless ways of practice?*

As long as we are sincerely practicing, progress and change naturally occur. Rather than seek these things we should enjoy the practice as we experience it. Training without joy and kindness leads to a hardened and bitter personality. This is incorrect practice.

Aikido cannot be taught; it is necessary to discover it within ourselves. If we are too full of ourselves, it is difficult to discover something new and subtle. Attempting to be as strong as possible, we may forget that it is self-control that solidifies understanding and ability.

At the beginning of training, it is very difficult to get rid of dependency on tightness and forcefulness—two habits that are detrimental to both health and spiritual development. For many students the beginning is the most difficult time and the time of the greatest personal confrontation. As our practice matures, we discover the inner power of ki as breath and mind. When we drop our defense mechanisms, the power of nature works through us and we feel unity with our environment. Our real substance, our will, stands up, and we become determined to eliminate the dualistic contradiction between ideals and everyday reality. Through practice, layers of delusion fall away and our innate powers of intuitive judgment are gradually roused from their long, deep sleep.

The effectiveness and refinement of our aikido technique, as of all our actions, is a barometer of our understanding of the aiki principle. Technique should be accomplished as economically as possible. As understanding increases, the need for hard exercise diminishes. Repetition *(renshu)* is important, but first of all it is essential that we grasp the meaning of *keiko*, the main word for practice.

KEIKO

The word *keiko* (lit., to think in the ancient way) means to perceive the way directly and intuitively. This is impossible until we are free of competitive mind; until we get beyond the idea of manipulating others. In traditional Japanese schools of swordsmanship, students were not allowed to spar with anyone outside their own dojo or style until they had received a certificate of proficiency. This was partly to avoid giving the impression that the school was of inferior quality, but also to insure that the student's progress would not be hindered by outside pressure and competitiveness.

■ *Keiko*

THE WAY OF
HARMONY

33

The high goals of aikido forbid the practice, and even the mentality, of competition. A competitive mind hinders the process of fine-tuning. Competition requires rules to insure the safety of the participants and this destroys a higher reality based on complete awareness. Budo can never become a form of sports. Proper respect includes an awareness of all the possibilities open to your opponent when you attack. You must be relaxed yet totally aware. Physical tightness as well as all ideas of success or failure must be dropped.

In Zen training, the absolute basis of reality is perceived by "dropping body and mind." A Zen monk came before the old master Joshu saying, "If I have nothing in my mind, what shall I do?" Joshu replied, "Throw it out!"[9] Dropping our defensiveness, the tension in our shoulders, is also a matter of mind. A person may have a flexible body, yet when confronted may still tighten up or react unreasonably. To drop mental and physical resistance is one and the same thing and neither can occur without deep faith and trust in ourselves.

The gradual discovery of a new kind of inner power makes possible the discarding of the old, protective mechanisms of the ego. The ability to remain calm in a threatening situation requires spiritual fortitude, lack of ego, and intimacy with one's real nature.

THE SPIRIT OF THE DOJO

The dojo (place for practice of the way) exists as a stable environment for practicing and manifesting the attitudes described above. Standing or sitting formally (seiza) alone in this sacred place, one experiences a great peace, a sense of oneness with nature and with those who have gone before on the path of self-development. When practice (keiko) begins, we become engrossed in the living study of aikido movement and all else is forgotten. Practicing the spontaneous manifestion of aikido principle, we experience our natural state of being. When we finish, we are refreshed, invigorated.

The aikido dojo exists today thanks to the efforts of those who have created and preserved the way since ancient times. In modern times this spirit was rekindled through the spiritual genius, dedication, and enlightenment of Morihei Ueshiba-sensei. The dojo is not a gymnasium or a place for the display of ego. It is a place that demands sincerity, respect, and humility—qualities essential for the safety and progress of each student.

So that students do not mistake the way, they must realize their obligations to themselves, their fellow students, the teacher, the dojo, and to aikido itself. In O-sensei's time, live-in students *(uchi deshi)* took care of the dojo and the needs of the master throughout the day and night. Their lifestyle was always under the scrutiny of the master. Today, however, the time spent in the dojo is only a few hours a day. In these busy times, a sincere commitment to practice is essential.

Aikido cannot be practiced conceptually. We need the honest resistance of a partner in order to study conflict-resolution. In aikido, as in Zen, though sudden insights are helpful they do not insure lasting ability or deep understanding. Experience teaches us not to grow attached to them. They are the crest of a wave of development. More important is the daily effort that builds body and mind. The goal of aikido is not sudden revelation but constantly to live from hara: to experience all of life with total body and mind and to manifest the joy and wonder of our natural state of being. It is not a path for seeking an individual or illusory salvation. Aikido is a spiritual path that requires years of training and refinement, not only of technique but of our entire being. Regular practice is necessary so that the spirit and understanding of aikido can continue to grow within us.

Observers of aikido are often surprised to see students practicing seriously, yet in a friendly manner. Excessive talking on the mat, however, is not acceptable. Words are not taboo, but they must not interupt *isshin-denshin,* the intuitive and direct transmission between teacher and student.

The tradition of the East is usually nonverbal, yet words have their place as guidelines for the student. Verbal explanations can never communicate the actual experience, ("The way that can be spoken of is not the constant way,"[10]), yet for Westerners, accustomed to detailed explanations, nonverbal teaching alone may be unacceptable. Even in Japan, few people today can understand or follow the nonverbal way exclusively.

Direct transmission is possible only when the student regularly receives personal attention from a teacher. In other words, it is difficult to teach aikido in large groups. Verbal teachings, although they may not be completely understood by the student at the time, lead the mind

■ *Reigi saho: Etiquette*

toward realization of basic principles. This resembles the use of apparently paradoxical questions or stories (koans) in Zen practice. In both Zen and aikido, realizing the meaning behind the words depends upon continual practice and reflection.

In aikido, there are many valuable key expressions: examples include *ashi mimi* (the ear of one's foot), *ashi moto* (in front of one's feet), *koshi ga suwaru* (to be well grounded, stable), *chikara wo nuku* (drop one's tightness). These are not long, drawn-out explanations yet they help students to discover the correct way of training. Even direct transmission is often facilitated with a well-chosen word or phrase that leads the student to break through a difficult problem. Attempting to understand the teachings left by ancient masters also helps students to understand their own experiences more deeply.

Verbal teachings thus provide a touchstone for the validity of experience. In the words of the Buddhist scholar Hee-Jin Kim, "In spite of inherent frailties in their makeup, words are the bearers of ultimate truth."[11] Speaking and going outward to help others is the ki of fire. This must be balanced by internal development, the ki of water. We should become like the Shinto deity *Omotaru no Kami*, constantly radiating spiritual energy outward to others, yet remaining full and complete within ourselves.

The object of ceremony is to curb arrogance. If we are overly confident or arrogant we will be easily defeated. Aikido requires receiving your partner's attack; blending with it in such a way that you have no weak point that can be attacked; and, when necessary, falling without injury. This is the art of *ukemi.* You must receive your partner's attack with an open yet impenetrable defense. A calm and sensitive awareness, free from arrogance or haughtiness, is developed by observing proper etiquette. Bowing correctly, for example, not only helps to eliminate self-centeredness but also teaches correct distance and timing *(ma-ai),* developing caution and judgment. One should not bow too low when the *ma-ai* is short. This indicates a lack of respect for your partner and invites his attack.

When entering the dojo, each person makes a standing bow to the front *(shomen),* where the shrine is located. Proper greeting is given to the teacher, seniors, and others. When leaving one should excuse oneself. Recognition of senior and junior student *(senpai-kohai)* relationships is essential to correct dojo etiquette. At the start of class, the teacher and students bow to each other and say in Japanese, *"Onegai shimasu*—I am making a request (for instruction)." At the end of the class everyone again bows and says, *"Arigato gozaimasu*—Thank you very much."

At the beginning of each class, both teacher and students, sitting formally *(seiza)* on their knees, bow to the front of the dojo, clap their hands twice and bow again. In some cases, when the dojo is within a Shinto shrine, everyone bows twice, claps twice, and then bows once more. The three bows symbolize the three origins: spirit, mind, and body. The clapping of the hands symbolizes the unity of the dynamic forces of nature. It also clears the mind of stagnation.

When our hands are placed together, the physical (the right side) and the spiritual (the left) parts of our constitution are united. In Buddhism, this gesture is called *gassho* and is often accompanied by bowing; in Christianity, it is the form of prayer. In aikido, as in Shinto, it is known as *musubi*, tying together the yin and the yang. All aikido movement is prayer, a method of uniting one's own will with that of universal will. In this regard, the founder, Morihei Ueshiba, stated,

Aikido begins and ends with formality.

The aikido master Seigo Yamaguchi was already an eighth *dan* (black belt) when I first met him. Some ten years later, shortly before leaving Japan, I attended one of his black-belt seminars *(kuro obi kai)*. At that time he passed out a pamphlet to each of the students. This is from the introduction to that pamphlet:

> At fifty-six years old I am beginning to reassess the real difficulty of Aikido. Truly it is necessary to always maintain beginner's mind. Merely by enthusiastically repeating those things which you have learned, you can in no way hope to gain true progress. It is true that the ancient masters were quoted as saying that one must train himself through continual repetition. This does not refer, however, to mechanical repetition.
>
> The ancient masters stated that we must not be content to pluck out only our bad habits. Our good habits as well, must be eradicated. Our bad habits, whether they are within our techniques or our everyday life and attitude, are easily recognized by all. Even

■ *Musubi*

■ *Shoshin: Beginner's Mind*

though they may seem to always be with us, nevertheless they are relatively easy to correct.

When we are aware of them they cause very little problem. Compared with this, our good habits are firmly assumed to be definite attributes and real virtues. The harmful effects of these are seldom realized. No matter how good we may believe we are, let us remain aware that we are still immature and imperfect. We should receive any and all criticism with a modest and unassuming feeling. To concentrate on becoming powerful and also maintain beginner's mind, is by no means an easy thing. Standing strong and firm without any hardness or inflexibility is the state of real positive spirit. It is all-accepting and yet never loses the consciousness of its own existence.

The depth of these words exemplifies the true spirit of aikido. Beginner's mind is not naive or lacking in conviction. It is to know oneself; to have eliminated doubts concerning the meaning of one's existence. Ueshiba-sensei once said,

Just like you, I am also on the way of my training.

Yet on another occasion he said,

Without me there is no aikido.

Such apparent contradiction was also found in the words of Japan's most legendary swordsman, Miyamoto Musashi. He claimed to have no teachers, yet said that everything was his teacher. Truth and contradiction are inseparable.

In the words of Ueshiba-sensei:

> *Takemusubi aiki is the mind that causes all the various intellectual approaches to cease. It is by no means a passive or conceptual endeavor. The way of the Japanese warrior is the way of the gods. It is a manifestation of the divine working of creation, which gave birth to heaven and earth. It is the manifestation of the god Izanagi and the goddess Izanami, the ancestors of humankind. The way of takemusubi aiki is to learn the law and order of the universe, the*

working of the cosmos, directly from the divine consciousness of
kannagara.

There is no room in aikido practice for conceptualization or opinion: no perfection, no right or wrong, only the reality of experience. We cannot claim to understand anything unless we actually can do it. This attitude underlies much that is traditional in Japanese society. It is expressed in the Zen koan, "When you meet a Zen master on the road, you cannot talk to him, you cannot face him with silence. What are you going to do?" The answer has to be in the spirit of, "Face him neither with words nor silence. Give him an uppercut!"[12] In other words, you must destroy the buddha: and this can be done only by becoming a buddha yourself.

In the practice of aikido, conflict and ego confrontation are replaced by intuition and wisdom. To quote O-sensei:

> *When practicing with one who has realized aikido principle within*
> *his being, all bad feelings and doubts are swept away and you gain*
> *a greater understanding of yourself."*

When the practitioner becomes accomplished mentally and spiritually, it is said that "Hara ga dekite iru—hara is finished." At this time, there is no longer any possibility of unreasonableness as a means of solving difficulties. Through aikido practice, life becomes joyful and deeply intuitive. We come to appreciate the ongoing process of self-development and to view challenges as opportunities. We realize that self-satisfaction destroys real progress and we learn to see the folly of seeking immediate gratification or instant success.

Each of us is the subjective center of the universe. We create our own lives, and each of us alone is responsible for whatever condition we find ourselves in. If there is something we are unhappy with, we must change ourselves. In Mahayana Buddhism this resolve to change is called faith. This is the kind of faith that comes only from experience and is a total acceptance of our own nature, just as we are. In esoteric Buddhism this attitude of acceptance is called "the wisdom that cultivates the will to practice compassion."

3 ▪ SHINTO: THE SPIRITUAL ROOTS OF AIKIDO

▪ *Shinto*

THE MYTHOLOGY OF SHINTO TELLS OF AN AGE before the dawn of history when all human beings were at one with universal law and possessed the consciousness of the gods. This age is known as *Kannagara*—suchness, or the flow of divine consciousness, pure and untouched by rationality or theory. In this consciousness is no question of divinity; one's own existence is proof of the divine nature of all things. Kannagara no michi is the history of consciousness manifesting itself through the evolution of the human mind. As James Mason, a Western explicator of Shinto, describes it:

> Primeval man was a self-conscious infant, but subconsciously, and
> in his responses to intuitive knowledge, he was more mature than
> modern man.[1]

The original attitude of human beings had two aspects: *itsugi*, at one with the dimensions of universal spirit; and *totsugi*, the creation and maintenance of human society according to the eight powers of yin and yang. The ancient Japanese saw the realms of life and death as a monistic dichotomy, both sides existing within *nakayima*, the present moment. This is subjective consciousness, the axis of time and space. *Kannagara no michi* is the life force evolving its own infinite potential. It is like the world of a small child, embracing everything and existing only as the present moment, here and now. Ueshiba-sensei explained:

> In ancient times, in the age of the gods, human beings were at one
> with the universal spirit. They were ara hito gami, manifest man
> gods. In those times they were aware of their nature as the divided
> spirits of the one great universal spirit.

In the early centuries C.E., the Japanese faith in kami came to be known as *Shinto*, the way of the gods. The Japanese reading of the Chinese *shin* is *kami*. Both words mean god, but they differ from the anthropomorphic idea, *God*, found in Western religions. *Ka* means fire, the energy of spiritualization (yang); and *mi* means water, the energy of materialization (yin). Kami (or shin) is the original spark of life, the spiritual control tower of consciousness. *To* is a shortened version of the Chinese *Tao*, the way. In other words, the foundation of Shinto is the creative energy of the universe, the kototama.

The kototama, creative life energy, functions within a unique principle of dualistic monism, yin and yang. It is a mistake to see yin and yang as separate forces; rather, they are two manifestations of a single force. Yin and yang together are pure polarity: a priori spirit. Being within, or of, all things, yet having no existence by themselves, they are called the "originally unborn." Yin and yang are infinity itself. Infinity is the source of absolute power, yet without yin and yang, the right and left hands of God, not one particle of energy in the world could be moved. Through the laws of the function of yin and yang, kototama (universal ki) continually manifests the material world.

Lao-tzu wrote in the *Tao Te Ching:* "The Tao generates one. One generates two. Two generates the three. The three generates all things."[2] Those words might also be expressed thusly: Oneness has two aspects, a back and a front. The constant and dynamic interchange between these polar opposites is the continual becoming of the threefold reality of all things. Yin and yang, continually born from the oneness of infinity, draw their life force from that mysterious source. Their constant interchange governs the creative energy of the universe and creates the kototama principle—the principle of aiki or universal harmony.

This is the principle that harmonizes all manifestation, visible and invisible. It is at play in all ideological and spiritual affairs and in our daily life as well. It is the one thing that does not change: it is the principle of change itself. Movement, consciousness, life, and God, are different expressions of the same reality. James Mason writes: "Shinto is a cult of ancestorship as an expression of the primeval subconscious intuition that mankind's ancestry makes man a descendent of Heaven, which means that man and divine spirit are the same." And again, "The true Shinto conception of heaven is not as a

■ *Kannagara no michi: The flow of consciousness*

■ *Figure 3.1: Life-will expanding as intuition*

spatial part of the universe, but spacelessness or subjectivity. . . ." In this sense, the history of the world, as of the universe at large, did begin in Heaven, the originating subjective center of divine creative spirit (the life-will) expanding objectively.[3]

Since ancient times, among so-called primitive people there has always been an instinctive feeling, an intuition, that all of nature is integrally grounded in and based on forces that are both complementary and antagonistic. These forces were understood as the function of oneness. This mysterious function of the yin/yang dynamic is the unique principle of aiki. It cannot be grasped conceptually, as one thing relative to another, subject to object, the seer to the seen. Attempting to grasp reality through concepts alone is like a group of blind men trying to describe an elephant: one speaks of the tail, another of the leg, and so on, while the whole escapes notice. Thus, it is impossible to fix a point where yin ends and yang begins. Aiki principle is known only experientially, through the elimination of opposites.

SHINTO MYTHOLOGY

As a creation of the human subconscious, Shinto is completely subjective and intuitive. It is both based on and predictive of the changing celestial influence of the stars. Shinto mythology maintains that the age of Kannagara existed in Taka Ama Hara, the high plain of heaven, until around fifteen thousand years ago, and that the world then was ruled by the sun goddess, Amaterasu Oh Mi Kami. The lineage of the sun (strict spiritualism) had seen the first world civilization, the time of the man-gods *(arahitogami)*, when people knew nothing of possessions, greed, or individual desires.

It is said that the gods first descended to Japan in the mountain highlands of Hida no Takayama. This may indicate a migration from a larger continent to the Japanese islands. The first god to descend was Ninigi no Mikoto, the grandson of Amaterasu Oh Mi Kami. He is credited with applying the spiritual principle of the kototama to society. Next followed the dynasty of Hikohohodemy, the golden age of prosperity, contemporary with the great civilizations of ancient Egypt and Sumer. Next came the age of Ugayafukiaezu, in which the ancient emperors toured the world teaching the spiritual principles of the kototama.

Finally, however, around the time of Jinmu Tenno (also the time of Moses), a new celestial influence began. It was now time for the sun god to step down and for the god of the moon (philosophy and materialism) to come into power. A great battle between Jinmu Tenno and Nigihayahi no Mikoto ensued. This was the beginning of the war between spiritualism and materialism, and it created karma that would continue for hundreds of generations into the future.

At the time of this great transition the leaders discussed among themselves how the change from spiritualism to materialism should be used for the creation of the future golden age. They agreed that, in spite of the karma that the human race would have to endure, it was necessary to hide the principles of spiritualism. As long as the people were aware of those principles, they would never develop the sense of competition necessary to create a materialist society, and the physical sciences would never develop far enough to prove the truth of spiritual principles. Lacking this material progress, the goal of creating a utopian society would be impossible. The Emperor Suijin (six centuries after the Jinmu restoration) understood this well and concealed the spiritual principles of the kototama at the grand shrine of Ise. This event was called the second closing of the rock door of heaven (ame no iwato).

Accordingly, when the kototama principle was hidden thousands of years ago, Shinto took on the forms and rituals of a religion. The Empress Amaterasu was deified as the goddess of the sun, with the mission of preserving the ancient teachings for the construction of a future golden age. Amaterasu's brother, Tsuki Yomi no Kami, became deified to rule over the area that was to become China. He took an image of the moon, symbolizing philosophy and religion, as his flag. The image of the stars symbolized the development of science and materialism, a responsibility no one wanted, and only after much discord was it accepted by Susa no Wo no Mikoto, the younger brother of Amaterasu.

When the ancient sun god retired, the people fried beans, so they would never sprout again, and threw them at the emperor, chanting, "Uchi wa fuku, oni wa soto (Let the strict goblin be cast out and individual freedom and happiness come in)." The frying of the beans meant that the strict realm of spiritual discipline would never rise again and that individual freedom (materialism) would continue forever. This sentiment remains alive today as a major weakness in the foundation of democracy. Individual rights, personal opinion, and material wealth are the predominant factors of modern society, taking precedence over responsibility, wisdom, humility, and spiritual training.

This piece of social engineering—creating people of competitive desire and establishing a society based on materialism—worked better than anyone had anticipated. People became so competitive and self-centered that they began killing each other en masse. Leaders became so superstitious and afraid of spiritual power that mighty kings slaughtered whole villages of newborn babes in order to avoid the birth of saints or spiritual leaders. Traces of this history remain in the stories of Moses and Jesus of Nazareth.

The tendency toward violent antispirituality picked up so much momentum that the threat of complete self-destruction was born. In the face of that tendency, saints and philosophers—the historical Buddha, Shakyamuni; Jesus; Lao-tzu; Confucius—came forth to meet the needs of those turbulent times. Recognizing the great difficulty of grasping spiritual truth, they taught through parables and symbols in order to reestablish humankind's spiritual direction.

The Buddha's student Ananda once asked, "What is Buddhism?" The holy one answered, "It is *shinnyo*, the likeness of truth." A Zen expression states, "Buddhism is a finger pointing at the moon," a reference to the individual sources of the kototama, which point to the ultimate reality of all existence.

Thus the direct spiritual understanding of the age of the gods gave way to philosophy and cosmology, and these, in turn, were succeeded by organized religion, which steered the direction of societies for several thousand years. Nowadays, the new religion is science; its god is wealth and power. When the atom was split and the atomic age became a reality, science tapped into the power of the invisible world, and misuse of this power threatens the existence of all terrestrial life. We have reached the time when the universal spiritual principles of the kototama must be revealed.

SHINTO TODAY

The teachings held by Amaterasu have been passed down from generation to generation through the education of the emperor and in the customs of the people. Shinto, by these means, became steeped in ritual; but strictly speaking, Shinto, even today, is not a religion. It has no canon or strict rules of behavior. Its philosophy and practice are based on customs passed down from antiquity. Shinto preaches no salvation, has no religious creed to which one can be converted, nor dogmatic teachings of right and wrong. Shinto does not preach morality or condemn souls for the lack of it. Nevertheless, the Japanese are a people of deeply religious feeling. All aspects of their traditional life involve prayer and ritual. Morality and judgment, considered inseparable, have been taught through budo and daily life. This was exemplified in the code of bushido, the traditional education of the aristocratic samurai class. The samurai felt responsible for even the most seemingly insignificant details of life. Failure to account for one's actions could result in death. They did not live by a rigid idea of right and wrong but rather with a sense of responsibility for their own judgment. They had little respect for abstract theory.

Shinto manifests in all aspects of Japanese life. *Japanese mind* is synonymous with *Shinto mind*. To Shinto mind, the divine is in all things. This mentality honors all of life and is expressed through respect for divine spirit, ancestors and all people, and the food we eat. It considers the earth and all of nature as living and conscious gods. Before people built shrines, rocks, trees, mountains, and objects of nature were worshiped. Some old cave shrines remain today, such as the Omiwa shrine in Nara prefecture and the Udo shrine on the island of Eno Shima near Kamakura. The sun, the source of existence, is worshiped as the manifestation of universal spirit. The heat and light of this ultimate deity represent the compassion and wisdom *(ai)* of the creator. In ancient times a priest would stand in front of a huge rounded rock, wave a branch of the sacred tree sakaki *(Cleyera ochnachea),* and chant Shinto invocations. The rock symbolizes the sacred mirror of Yata, the spirit of Amaterasu Oh Mi Kami, the sun goddess. The real deity behind the mirror, however, is Naobi, our direct spirit. In Shinto, Naobi is also called Ame no Mi Naka Nushi, the divine ruler of the center of heaven—that is, of the space wherein reside the life-will and power.

伊勢神宮

Both the fine and the martial arts of Japan express kannagara, the tao. The Shinto view holds that the invisible world of spirit is the basic reality, and the physically manifest world *(utsushiyo)* is a reflection of the invisible. Whatever happens in the realm of mind (the fourth dimension) inevitably manifests in the material world as well. The genius of primitive mind seeks the truth of reality by going deep into the experience of the present moment. This is seen in all aspects of Japanese society and art including the tea ceremony *(chado)*, flower arrangement *(ikebana),* and aikido. O-sensei's spiritual teacher Deguchi Wanisaburo explicitly taught that the martial and fine arts of Japan were ways to merge with the divine consciousness. To manifest the perfection of the kototama in the material world is *kamiwaza* or "divine technique," a term also used to describe O-sensei's techniques.

ISE SHRINE

In addition to using caves and rocks as places of worship, the Japanese build shrines in many, many places. While there are many famous and beautiful shrines, small humble shrines are to be found almost anywhere. Family gardens often hold shrines; hiking in the mountains, you will find them by small streams. For the Japanese, God is life itself and exists in everything, or *is* everything. To claim that people are descendent of the gods is another way of saying that humankind is a manifestation of the divine flow of consciousness, the kototama.

Shinto is not limited to Japan: it encompasses the entire history of human existence. Anyone who lives in accordance with natural law (that is, anyone who realizes the compassion of the great creator spirit) is a living embodiment of Shinto. Japanese people are born Shintoist because their language, and therefore their society, expresses Shinto mind, the kototama.

Although the kototama is integrated into the everyday Japanese life, its principles, concealed since ancient times, have long since been forgotten. The majestic shrines of Shinto today stand silent, maintaining the secrets that now continue mainly as ritual and symbolic tradition. The Grand Shrine of Ise, in Mie prefecture, is now the main shrine in Japan. The imperial household has visited Ise shrine for centuries. The inner shrine *(naiku)* and the outer shrine *(geku)* have a recorded history of almost two thousand years. By tradition, no decision of great importance to the country of Japan is made without first being placed in prayer before this shrine.

Amaterasu Oh Mi Kami, the sun goddess enshrined at Ise's inner shrine, and Toyoke no Oh Mi Kami, the god of the earth enshrined at the outer shrine, are the two main deities of Shinto. This symbolism illustrates the direct connection of Shinto with nature. The sun represents the world of spirit; the earth represents the vegetal basis of existence, supporting physical life.

The Ise shrine buildings are simple. They are built of unpainted Japanese cypress (*hinoki*, lit., the ki of spirit) procured from imperial forests in the Kiso Mountains. The architecture is the pure Japanese traditional style that prevailed long before the introduction of Chinese-style construction (figure 3.2). The grand shrine itself has a traditional thatched roof, called *kayabuki*. The buildings are dismantled and rebuilt on adjoining plots every twenty years in a ceremony called *sengu-shiki*.

The kototama is symbolized throughout the shrine grounds. The river that runs though the grounds is called Isuzu Gawa, the river of fifty bells, symbolizing the vibrations of universal creation. In Shinto,

■ *Figure 3.2: Traditional Japanese shrine architecture*

the fifty pure sounds of the kototama, from which all words are derived, are seen as individual deities. All language expresses the kototama, but Japanese preserves its original principle very clearly. Each sound of the Japanese syllabary is a deity that serves a particular function in the creative evolution of the universe. The five vowels represent the universal dimensions, while the consonants express the eight powers of yin and yang through which these dimensions manifest.

The bridge over the river is called Uji Bashi, the bridge where the universal law presides. It faces a huge forest through which water runs down from the mountains, symbolizing the eternal flow of life. The roof contains ten logs, one for each of the ten rows of the kototama syllabary (I Hi Si Ti Ki Mi Yi Ri Ni Wi). The entrance gate is called a *torii* (lit., bird place), but the kototama of Torii means the life-will (I) crossing over or passing through (toru) from the spirit world (subjective, A I E O U) to the manifest realm (objective, Wa Wi We Wo Wu).

In figure 3.3 it will be seen that *A* and *Wa* are the subjective and objective sides of a single dimension. The same is true of *O-Wo* and *E-We*. In *The Gospel According to Thomas*, the vowel dimensions are called the tree of life and the semivowels are called the tree of wisdom. "For you have five trees in paradise which are unmoved in Summer or in Winter, and their leaves do not fall. Whoever knows them shall not taste death."[4] In Shinto, they are Ame no Mihashira, the divine pillar of heaven, and Kuni no Mihashira, the divine pillar of earth.

The crossbeam, originally a braided rope *(shimenawa)* connecting the two pillars, represents the spiraling energy connecting body and spirit. This is a momentary synapse or spark of life in which the Eight Powers manifest consciousness and existence. The original bird of the torri was the *Niwatori* (garden bird; a chicken), which was honored as the bird that faces the sun. It shows us the directions of the compass and calls us to awaken. In the mythological records of the *Kojiki,* the bird of the torii is referred to as "the sandpiper that flies to and fro on the island of Awa." In the western tradition it is the stork which brings new life into this world. Some other legends consider the crow as the bird which carries souls between this world and the next.

Within the main shrine is the sacred mirror of Yata, the symbol of infinity. The mirror is said to have been passed down to the emperor Ninigi no Mikoto, the grandson of Amaterasu, from the sun goddess herself. The inner shrine is open only to the Japanese emperor, who is

Objective consciousness									Subjective consciousness
Matter									Mind
Passive									Active
Wi	Ni	Yi	Ri	Mi	Ki	Si	Ti	Hi	I
We									E
Wu									U
Wo									O
Wa									A

■ Figure 3.3: Torii: The entrance gate between spirit and matter. Photo by Larry Lieberman.

educated in the ancient teachings of his ancestors. He is not a despotic monarch but rather a symbol of unity for the Japanese people. Since World War II he has also been considered a symbol of the state, yet his mission is to live according to the teachings of his ancestors and, through his example, bring about world peace and harmony. In Japanese tradition, he represents the divine origin of the human race and preserves the way of the gods that it may be realized on earth.

Kannagara is the flow of nature, the seasons of the year, and the unfolding of human destiny. It is the evolution of the universe as both matter and consciousness. There is no absolute beginning. This feeling is celebrated in Japan's annual festivals. The new year in Japan honors the past and prepares for the future. It is a time for sharing and for families to get together. The feeling resembles that of Christmas in the Christian world, and the festival even has similar symbols.

The Japanese god of wealth and spiritual happiness, Oh Kuni Tama Oh Kuni Nushi, resembles the Christian community's Saint Nicholas. He brings gifts of wealth to the people, symbolizing the distribution of spiritual prosperity or happiness. Although Christmas trees as such are rarely seen in Japan, the Japanese place a somewhat similar meaning on the pine tree. Pine branches and wreaths are placed on the doors of houses and even sometimes on the front of automobiles to protect them for the new year. The pine tree in Japanese is called *matsu*, "to wait"—not unlike the English expression to "pine" for someone. Christmas celebrates the fulfillment of a prophecy, the birth of Christ. The pine symbolizes another prophecy, the coming of a golden age for humanity. In Japan, the new year is a time to purify one's feeling as a means of inviting divine spirit to manifest on earth.

Shinto cosmology and mythology tell us that we are now experiencing the difficulties of the birth of a new golden age. The past several thousand years has been the time of materialism. In the process of creating the physical sciences and the raising of intellectual ability, humankind has endured much poverty of the spirit. Countless people have died in wars and suffered from fear and superstition. The karma of the past must be swept away, and people of all races must again embrace as one family.

Spirit is the ruler of life; mind follows, and the body is the temple of both. We have passed through the ages of spirituality and of philosophy and are now drawing to the end of the age of materialism. The time of waiting for the golden age is over; the birth is at hand. The new child must be ushered into the world by our final and best efforts.

This new age requires the purification *(misogi)* of the earth and mankind. To oppose this great misogi is to oppose michi, the way, and will only intensify the difficulty of this intense purification.

The power for this purification comes from the deity Murakumo Kuki Samuhara Ryuoh Oh Kami, the dragon god who severs delusion and eliminates the accumulated karma of the ages. The sword of Murakumo is called *kusanagi no tsurugi. Kusa* is grass or weeds, the worthless overgrowth of karma produced by civilization; *nagi* or *tsurugi* is the long sword or scythe that severs this karma, scattering it in the winds of the eight directions. This mission of purification is carried out by Take Haya Susa no Wo no Mikoto, who is known in Shinto mythology as a wild, jealous, mischievous god. He is also the god of budo.

O-sensei felt that the mission of Susa no Wo no Mikoto was his personal mission and that aikido was the means for carrying out the great purification. He referred to this mission with the words:

> *Aiki is the sword of Susa no Wo, the body of Ki.*

To grasp O-sensei's point fully requires an appreciation of the Shinto story of *Ame no Iwato Biraki*, the opening of the rock door of heaven.

Susa no Wo no Mikoto had been given the mission of developing materialism and purifying the karma created in that process, but he refused and was banished from Taka Ama Hara, the heavenly world. Upset, he started a quarrel with his sister Amaterasu and later skinned a horse alive and threw the bloody hide among the women who were weaving kimono in Amaterasu's house. At this, Amaterasu became distraught and hid herself in a cave behind a rock door. This caused the sun to disappear from Taka Ama Hara and Ashi Hara (the earthly world) as well. The world entered into eternal night, and the evil gods took advantage of this situation by throwing the world into chaos. In order to remedy this tragic situation, the gods had a meeting and decided to stage a huge celebration. They asked the goddess Ame no Uzume no Mikoto to perform an erotic dance. This made all the gods laugh and shout with great joy. Inside the cave, Amaterasu, hearing the commotion, wondered how there could be happiness in the world without her light and went to the door to ask what was going on. Told that there was another deity much greater than her, in jealousy she peeked out to see—only to be dazzled by her own reflection in a mirror that had been placed at the door. At that moment she was caught by Ame no Tajikara Wo no Kami, a god of great strength, who pulled her back into the world.

O-sensei referred to this story saying,

> *Aikido is the second opening of Ame no Iwato* [the rock door of heaven].

Because the world is not yet united as one family in peace, the job of Susa no Wo no Mikato remains unfinished. Violence in the world has caused the light of love and wisdom to become hidden behind the rock door of human consciousness. Now is the time for the dance of the gods, aikido, to bring about the second opening of Ame no Iwato. When the Eastern world sees its own light of spiritual power reflected in the West, it will reemerge as a power for peace. In O-sensei's words:

> *Iwato Biraki is to create a society in which the body is used as a tool to accomplish the mission of the soul and spirit. Establishing orderliness in your breath, bring your ki under control, and plant your feet firmly on the path of self-realization. With this foundation, practice the techniques of takemusu aiki and bring the actual body of the universe into your breath.*

■ *Kado matsu: Waiting for divine spirit*

WAITING FOR DIVINE SPIRIT

When the Japanese place pine wreaths on their doors for the new year, it is called *kado matsu*, (*kado*, door; *matsu*, pine). The kototama of *Ka* means "spirit"; *do* (from *to*) means "to stop" or "to break through to spiritual understanding." *Ma* is sincerity or reality; *tsu* is to cycle toward materialization; hence, matsu is the vibration of the human spirit pushing forward against any and all difficulties to manifest peace and happiness on this earth. It is waiting for the spiritual evolution and reunification of the world's people. Thus, kado matsu means "waiting for divine spirit to stop" at the house where the wreath is hung.

There is a famous meeting place at Shibuya station in Tokyo, that is marked by a statue of a dog named Hachiko. Hachiko used to meet his master, a retired colonel, there every day. When his master died, Hachiko unknowingly continued to go there and wait for him. People tried to feed him, but he would not accept food from anyone, wanting only his master, and he finally starved to death. The people of the area were so moved by the sincere devotion of Hachiko that they erected a statue of him. Today it has become a famous meeting place for people in the heart of metropolitan Tokyo (see figure 3.4).

Such is the heart of makoto: waiting with fierce determination for the

dream of mankind to manifest. It is nurturing something inside that has almost completely been forgotten—our origin and spiritual birthplace.

Japanese Buddhists say, "Kawa wa taezu nagareru, shikamo. . . —the flow of the river is constant, yet. . . ." The changes of life (the flow) are constant, but the real self (the river) is everpresent. Within change there is something that does not change. This unmoving will, nurturing one absolute purpose, waiting for it to materialize, is the spirit of Shinto. It is expressed in the phrase that is repeated at the end of almost all Shinto prayers:

> *Kannagara tamahi chihaimase.*
> *Kannagara tamahi chihaimase.*
>
> May the divine spirit of the universe flourish
> throughout this world.

Morihei Ueshiba expressed this desire through his creation of aikido. As a manifestation of the kototama, the original principle of universal order, it embodies *ai*, love and wisdom, and is a tool for the creation of world peace.

4 ▪ KOTOTAMA: THE WORLD OF KI

▪ *The Word Souls*

THE KOTOTAMA IS THE ENERGY OF LIFE AND CREATION. It is the final indivisible energy of the universe that creates the form and function of universal spirit *(ki),* including the human spiritual constitution. The five vowels, A I E O U, or mother sounds, are the a priori dimensions of the universe, preceding both vibration and audible sound. The eight consonants, Hi Ni Si Ri Ti Yi Ki Mi, or father rhythms, are the rhythms of yin and yang, the point from which polarity and vibration begin. When the mother sounds and the father sounds combine, they create the actual vibrations behind all manifestation. This is the language of the spheres: consciousness itself. It is the constant reality behind change, the beginningless beginning. Unconditioned by time and space, it is always here and now, that which is closest to you, you yourself. It permeates the world of form and immerses you in the ocean of infinity. The infinite mother is always pregnant with the world of form. In Shinto, the kototama is called *shin rei kai,* the divine spiritual world; the realm of the gods.

In many cultures, words were traditionally considered sacred, and how they were used was thought to create or destroy a person's spiritual power and strength of character. It was so in Japan. The Japanese literary classic *The Manyoshu* refers to Japan as *kototama no sakiwau kuni* (the country where the soul of language flourishes). It has also been called *koto age no shinai kuni* (the land where words are not used for discussion or dispute). The existence of divine spirit is rarely questioned in Japan. Because I feel love, gratitude, and virtue in my heart, divinity exists. This feeling so thoroughly permeates the soul of Japan that even today the Japanese people still dislike detailed explanations. Traditional practices are always taught by example rather than with words or logic.

The kototama exists only as expressed through the form, function, and feeling of the relative world. Each kototama, whether spoken, thought, or expressed through movement, influences us both physically and spiritually. In the world's religions, the power of kototama is experienced through chanting and prayer. Studying movement as spirit and consciousness is also the study of the kototama. O-sensei created aikido based on the kototama principle:

Aikido is the superlative way to practice the kototama. It is the means by which one realizes his true nature as a god and finds ultimate freedom.

In the human ability to use the kototama for thought and speech lies the potential for absolute freedom. Yet if we do not realize that huge potential, much of our effort is wasted and we create little of lasting value. In the words of Emerson, "Man is nature made conscious." Human beings did not create language. The language of the spheres (kototama) created human beings and became innate human ability. Whatever achievements may be credited to humankind, we are still the receivers *(ukemi)* of life. By using consciousness, seekers try to discover the origin of that consciousness.

Without the kototama, the abstract thought and creativity necessary for this search would be impossible. Animals have their sounds or cries (*otodama*, "spirit of sound"), but being unable to use the kototama to direct their consciousness, they cannot control their own spiritual destiny. The progress of humanity depends on the evolution of intuitive judgment and the language with which it is expressed, for judgment and language determine the quality of any society.

THE VOWEL DIMENSIONS

The a priori world occurs on five levels or dimensions; these are the levels of human realization. Each level is represented in the kototama by a vowel, indicating subjective reality; preceded by a *W*, that vowel indicates objective reality. The first level is U, our sense of pure existence, and Wu, our physical senses. This level divides into A and Wa, our sense of self and other. From A-Wa comes O-Wo and E-We, the realms of memory and judgment and their objective capacities. When substance is understood as the life-will and power (I-Wi), we manifest the kototama of Ya,

有
無

- *U-Mu: The infinite void*

or Ia: wisdom and compassion, at one with the universal spirit. This is to stand on *ame no uki hashi*, the floating bridge of heaven. Individual will merges with that of the universe and creativity begins.

The Infinite Void: The U Dimension

The quality of our language creates the quality of society and assists in the evolution of consciousness. This process begins with the dimension of U, the void. There is something there but it cannot be recognized or named. Our senses are functioning, but as of yet, no consciousness of self and other exists. Ueshiba-sensei stated,

> The foundation of aikido is within becoming empty like the sky. From this standpoint, the freedom of harmonious movement is born. Becoming empty means to discard all illusory thinking and mistaken ideas of self. The highest consciousness (gokui) of aikido is to blend one's movement with the invisible world of spirit, the kototama. This being accomplished the entire universe is contained in your hara, the vital center from which new life energy is born. Through budo I have become enlightened to this reality.

To become empty; to stand in the void: What does this mean? *Hanya Shingyo* (*The Heart Sutra* of Buddhism) states, "Ku soku ze shiki, shiki soku ze ku—Emptiness is form, form is emptiness." This is the U dimension. Far from being empty, it is the absolute basis of reality. In this reality, there is no separation between self and other. In the words of Zen master Dogen, "To study the self is to forget the self; to forget the self is to be enlightened by the ten thousand things."[1]

O-sensei described this state as "no-mind," *mushin*—being free of all ego delusions that separate us from the heart and mind of the creator spirit of the universe, the kototama of Su. Emptiness, expressed in this way, is oneness with the universe. It is not to be understood by looking outside of ourselves, but by allowing the outside world to come to us and prove our existence.

O-sensei created aikido, which has been called moving Zen, as a means of accomplishing this. In aikido we learn not to become over-extended in attempting to control our partner, but to let him come into our sphere of influence until there is no separation. In this way our partner's power becomes our own. As our training matures, excessive conceptualization and the defense mechanisms of the ego gradually and naturally fade away.

The U dimension is the simultaneous reality of gross matter and pure spirit as one and the same energy. It is the absolute basis of reality and it is our spirit, *naobi*, at one with that of the universe. The vibration of U, associated with the corpus callosum, the midbrain, and the brain stem, is the source of both our automatic and intuitive functions. It creates our senses (Wu) and thereby our sense of existence, the finite and three-dimensional universe *(uchu)*. Mu, the invisible life-force of that existence, is the infinite, three-dimensional world. The interreaction between U and Mu creates *umu*, the power of birth. The noun form of *umu* is *umi*, which means "ocean," the birthplace of life on this planet. In Shinto, this spiritual energy is represented by the deity Ubusuna, who governs birth and productivity.

The Eastern view of creation is not that the world was created by an anthropomorphic god but that the universe gave birth to itself. We are both matter and spirit: there is no separation between the one who sees and the one who is seen. The Buddhist saint Kukai likened the voice of U to space, which is in want of nothing; space that contains Buddha nature. U stands for that which meets no obstacles, knows no decrease, and is originally uncreated: the transcendance of relativity. Kukai:

> This is what is called a great loss.
> Yet the one with Four Forms and Three Mysteries,
> The one too great to depict, even if we used
> The earth for ink and Mount Sumeru for brush,
> Is perfect and eternally present without change;
> This is indeed the ultimate meaning of the letter [U].[2]

The following expression of Lao-tzu's is very close in feeling to Kukai's:

> Is not the space between heaven and earth like a
>   bellows?
> It is empty without being exhausted.
> The more it works the more comes out.[3]

Modern science describes the U dimension as an electromagnetic energy field that contains and controls material existence. This is the kototama of Ku and Mu, absolute dryness and unconditional electromagnetic energy or ki. As Fritjof Capra notes, "the void of the Eastern mystics can easily be compared to the quantum field of subatomic physics."[4] This field is the realm of ki, or life energy itself. The seemingly empty space of the universe (U dimension) is full to overflowing with ki and is always in a state of tension. In Shinto, this a priori realm is called *gokubikai*, the infinitesimal world. "Ki is the foundation or source of the relative world, much like the atoms were once considered the basic substance of matter. As such, all manifestations of nature, including the more subtle qualities of emotion, mind, and spirit, are products of Ki."[5]

The world of matter appears to be solid, yet even the great mountains are nothing but a swirling mass of energy. We live in a sea of constant transition; birth, growth, prosperity, death: the cycle is repeated endlessly. "All our concepts (including those of space and time) are merely creations of the mind."[6] The material world of cells and atoms is continually breaking down and rebuilding, but the life-field, the invisible reality behind matter and form, guides the constant reconstruction of matter and maintains its shape and form.

The molecules and physical cells of our bodies are constantly changing. Old cells die and, owing to our field of ki, new cells are continuously created to replace the old ones. Every seven years one's entire body is completely renewed. There is not one cell that was there before. The practice of aikido rebuilds the field of ki according to universal order. There is no limit to the possible rebuilding and improvement of one's spiritual and physical constitution.

This ki field, life force, is wisdom *(prajna)* itself. No one has more ki than anyone else. One life is no more or less than any other. It is our intuitive judgment and how we use it that makes a difference.

In Shinto, the essence of the kototama is represented by the three sacred treasures and the deities associated with them. The three treasures are the mirror, the sword, and the beads. The word for mirror, *kagami*, also means "to see oneself through the eyes of God." This is self-reflection from the view of supreme judgment, the enlightened mind. It is the wisdom of makoto, which sees reality without judging or comparing. The three sacred treasures also correspond to sangen, the three origins. The mirror corresponds to the square: the love and wisdom (Ai) of Amaterasu Oh Mi Kami, the universal spirit, expanding infinitely. The perfection of the bright

■ *The Mirror*

| Ka | Ga | Mi |

| God | Self | See |

mirror mind of Amaterasu originates in the void. The sacred mirror of Shinto, called *Yata no Kagami*, is kept in the main shrine at Ise.

The kototama of Ya represents energy released outward in eight directions and traveling instantaneously to infinity. Pushing on its own center, Ta (the power of contrast) creates movement outward in all directions and forms a perfect sphere of ki energy. This is the electromagnetic field of universal breath *(kokyu)* or spirit. In aikido, the expansive power of kokyu (Ya) is also created in this way by pushing inward on ourselves rather than outward on our partner. Real power and freedom of movement depend on self-awareness, regardless of outside circumstances.

The mirror of Yata radiates the infinite love and wisdom of universal spirit outward in all directions. The expansion of pure polarity creates Tama, the perfect sphere of spirit. The life-will and power (I-Wi) are the center of this sphere. Combined they are Yi, the mountain of wisdom, the unification of individual and universal will. In Shingon Buddhism it is said, "Buddhas are said to have realized enlightenment because the mind is like a bright mirror set on a high stand, reflecting all images. The faultless, bright mirror mind of Mahavairochana [the great sun buddha], being placed on the summit of the world of dharma, calmly illumines all beings."[7]

The spirit behind the sacred mirror of Yata is the kototama of Su. Su supports U (Ame no Mi Naka Nushi, the deity of the center), the infinite void or vacuum. Su and U are the direct spirit of the universe and our own direct spirit as well. From the U dimension, all other kototama are born, and all, in turn, eventually return to this infinite void.

In the words of O-sensei:

> The kototama of U is the form of eternal prosperity within nothingness—no heaven, no earth, only the expanse of the infinite vacuum. From within this oneness comes the first spark of life and consciousness. From that point, infinitesimal particles of ki radiating life energy begin to map out a larger circle around this first spark. The result is the birth of the kototama of Su, the beginningless beginning of the universe. The biblical expression "In the beginning was the word" refers to this kototama. When one understands the working of spiral energy and trains oneself in the truth of the spirit, aiki is created.

YA
Eight

TA
Field

▪ *Yata: The power of contrast*

▪ *The creator god of Su*

The expansion of U leads to its division into A and Wa, yet our A dimension's consciousness cannot detect the original spark of life that makes consciousness itself possible. This spark is the life-will (I-Wi), the motive power of life, which stabilizes our mind and brings it under control. To realize I-Wi fully is to merge with universal will, to unify heaven and earth.

The Life-Will and Power: The I Dimension

The control center and motive power of the creator god (Su) is the I dimension: Izanagi no Kami (I) and Izanami no Kami (Wi), the first spiritual ancestors of mankind. They are the creative impetus of life—the power of verticality without which neither consciousness nor matter could be established.

意

• I

井

• Wi

This has been explained by James Mason as follows: "Between life (ki) and matter there must be a subjective coordination implying a common source. Otherwise life could not turn matter into a living being." Considered together, life and matter are called *izanagi oh mi kami*, the life-will. The life-will is virtue itself; it should not be confused with desire, nor with individual willpower, which is only the tip of the iceberg of our real substance. Mason describes this power as "the spontaneous impulse of life seeking freedom of action. Because of the way it has shown competence to mold life and matter during the long course of evolution, it must be aware of subjective reality. It must have a direct knowledge of life. It is, in fact, life's knowledge, self-evolving its own competence as it creates."[8]

The voice of I stimulates the central lobe of the brain and is associated with perception and sensitivity. It unites heaven and earth (spirit and body) through humankind's vertical posture. Conflict and difficulty are the meeting of opposing forces without a unifying factor or catalyst through which they can be harmoniously united. This third factor is will itself. It is the motive power of life, yet remains concealed. It is called *kakurigami*, a hidden deity.

Infinite Expansion: The A Dimension

The kototama of A holds the power of infinite expansion. Infinite expansion is the personification of the void. The expansion (A) and the center (I) of the U dimension are the love and wisdom (the heat and light) of Amaterasu, the sun goddess. Amaterasu is sometimes personified as the trinity Ame no Mi Naka Nushi (U), Takami Musubi no Kami (A), and Kami Musubi no Kami (Wa). These three deities represent both the polarization of the void into subjective and objective consciousness and wisdom manifesting as mercy (yin) and compassion (yang). O-sensei called this trinity *iki miya*, the living shrine of the human body.

In ancient Shinto, Izanagi Oh Mi Kami (I-Wi) held the distinguished position of *amatsu gami*, the deity of heaven. This title was transferred to the sun goddess Amaterasu (A), and Izanagi Oh Mi Kami came to represent universal principle.

In Shinto, the individual soul is said to be a division of Amaterasu, whose Hindu counterpart is called *atman*—soul or universal self. A is the beginning, the light of consciousness. It lights up the void of instinctive mind and reveals the manifest world. The kototama of A stimulates the frontal lobe of the brain, producing imagination, aspiration, abstraction, and gratitude. We realize it objectively as Wa, spiritual capacity.

Judgment and Courage: The E Dimension

The Japanese word for sword is *katana* or *tachi. Katachi*, or simply, *Kata*, is form and *na* is name, the kototama itself. *Katana* is the particular kototama which begins the creation of universal form. The word *tachi* may be seen as the short for katachi. The kototama taking form is the birth of the relative world. Lao Tsu: "The named was the mother of the myriad creatures." The power behind the sword is that of the *E* dimension, the *tsurugi*, or double edge sword of judgment and courage. This is the source of *misogi* or spiritual purification which allows us to create images in our mind and also creates the exterior form of the universe.

Just as water purifies itself by constant running, we continually reevaluate the memories that we use for present judgment. This evaluation is the fire (E) of misogi that gives people the courage to change their lives. E disperses energy rather than accumulating it. It manifests as We, judgment capacity and creativity. It is the intensity of the E dimension that leads people toward the discovery of their substance, the life-will (I). The life-will continually strives to manifest its own perfect wisdom (IE) through the evolution of human consciousness. With the life-will (I) as center, our judgment (E) becomes more refined and economical until, like a spinning egg, consciousness stands up as IE—supreme judgment or satori.

■ *The Sword*

加　　田　　名

Ka　　Ta　　Na

This kototama stimulates the parietal lobe in the brain, enabling the individual to perceive the ultimate justice of nature's laws. Nahum Stiskin writes: "Nature is constant process and the movement that constitutes it is the perfect execution of the all encompassing law of universal order."[10] Through the power of the E dimension, judgment improves, activity becomes more economical, and the practitioner gains effortless power and control—what Lao-tzu termed nondoing.

In the *Kojiki* (the book of ancient happenings) this kototama is represented as the swordsman in the sky swinging his sword (judgment) freely in all directions. The master swordsman divides heaven and earth without creating the slightest separation. He makes the two exist as one. This is the virtue of supreme judgment, the kototama of IE. This sword of judgment is the only thing human beings can depend on. It is represented in the Bible as salt, the essence of the physical world: "You are salt to the world. And if salt becomes tasteless, how is its saltness to be restored."[11]

The divine sword is double-edged. It creates both harmony and discord. It cuts through delusion and can raise the individual to new levels of understanding. "When the sword works horizontally it creates knowledge and division. When it is used vertically it creates the universal dimensions and unification."[12] By the power of judgment, universal law is perceived and individual progress begins.

In Western society, the sword of judgment mainly works horizontally, producing the idea that all men are created equal but separate. This materialistic view of life considers animal nature to be basic to the human race and spiritual essence to be only an ideal. In reality we are neither equal nor separate. We are individual energy centers within the great net of universal spirit. If we understand ourselves as divisions of this one great spirit, a society of health, harmony, and prosperity becomes possible.

Beauty and Self-Organization: The O Dimension

The outgoing energy of E (fire) creates form. O (water), manifests ki, the inner content of form. O is the power of connection, continuation, and accumulation. This energy is symbolized by the *magatama*, an ancient Shinto meditation object consisting of 365 beads strung together to represent the changing electromagnetic field of the earth as it makes its annual journey around the sun. Interspersed among the 365 beads are four red beads showing the four seasons. A large gray bead, which rests at the

■ *Magatama*

back of the neck when the beads are worn, represents the seven stars of the Big Dipper in the constellation of Ursa Major, the Great Bear. Opposing this is another large gray bead representing the earth, which rests on the chest. To the right and left of the earth bead are red beads symbolizing the sun and the moon. When used in prayer, the beads show the revolution of the sun and moon in relation to the earth over the period of a year.

Tama is spirit, a circular field of ki or life energy. *Maga* indicates that this sphere has become elongated by relative movement. As this energy pattern is the same as that of the human fetus, the magatama also symbolizes the spiritual energy that manifests human form (figure 4.1). As the mirror represents reality *(makoto; shin)* and the sword represents virtue and courage *(zen; yu),* so do the beads symbolize beauty *(bi),* the ki of the manifest world. The symbolism of the magatama as creative energy is paralleled in Buddhism and Christianity in the form of prayer or rosary beads.

 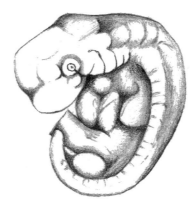

■ *Figure 4.1. Magatama and human fetus*

O creates physical health through the strengthening of ki. The voice of O stimulates the temporal lobe and cerebellum, producing volition and action. It manifests as Wo: instinct, memory, and the capacity for knowledge.

The vowel dimensions work together to create both the world of physical elements and the individual's ki fields. Undifferentiated energy (universal ki) fills the empty space of the U dimension. Unable to disperse this ki, the life-will (I dimension) creates a direction of movement toward a center. In this way, the universal vacuum (U) gathers all the necessary ingredients for life's continuance. Judgment (E) divides and selects this incoming energy, choosing only those ingredients best suited for the creation of each part of the human body. Infinite expansion (A), meeting with itself (Wa), creates resistance and spirals of materialization are born at the geometrical point of bifurcation. The E dimension gives this energy form and the O dimension ties that form tightly together by filling it with ki or life energy. The more this ki travels toward the center of its own spiral, toward materialization, the greater the resistance it encounters and, like an ocean wave going toward the beach, the more physically powerful it becomes. In this way, ki energy continually creates the world of physical elements.

Ki is spirit and it is the essence of the material world as well. Just as water expands when it freezes, the manifest world is a frozen and expanded state of ki energy. It appears to be solid, but in reality it is emptiness. The conversion of ki into form is primarily the function of the O dimension, the ki of water. Where water exists, life and nature flourish. The O dimension creates and preserves physical health through which the thread of will (I) gives vitality. When life forms lose the ki of water, due to an excess of fire ki (E), they contract and die and their life force (I) returns to the U dimension from which it originated.

A similar interrelational process between the vowel dimensions occurs within the brain, giving birth to individual consciousness. Instinct or memory (O) supports judgment and creative thought (E), as well as intuitive perception (I). The I dimension is the thread that strings the elements of soul and spirit (tama) together. The E dimension promotes spiritual growth.

In philosophical terms, universal principle is expressed as yin and yang. The balance of the yin/yang dynamic can be understood through the kototama. O, symbolized by water, sinks downward and creates the material (frozen) world. It has a feeling both of greatness and power (yang) and also flexibility, gentleness, and grace (yin). I is the central factor of balance and stability. Its contracted (yang) energy creates intuition and sensitivity (yin). E is more ethereal, mental energy (yin), yet it is extremely active and produces heat (yang). A is the most relaxed and expanded (yin) energy. It generates the birth of new life and manifestation (yang). U is the most balanced.

• *Yin*

• *Yang*

AMATSU IWASAKA

The first seventeen sounds of the kototama are a priori. They are *amatsu iwasaka*, the foundation of the human spiritual condition (see table 4.1). Considered separately, they have no real existence. Together they are interpreted as universal order, michi, the divine mission that human beings must fulfill. In the Chinese classic of divination, the *I-Ching*, this a priori world is called *sen ten*—"before heaven." It is shown as four pairs of opposing factors represented in the trigram arrangement of Fsu Hsi (see chapter 6).

■ *Amatsu Iwasaka*

TABLE 4.1
The Seventeen Sounds of Amatsu Iwasaka

			U				
	A		—		Wa		
O		—	E	We		—	Wo
Hi	Ti	Si	Ki	Mi	Ri	Yi	Ni
	I		—	Wi			

Source: Ogasawara, *Kototama Hyakushin*, 56.

Until the realization of our actual substance (I dimension), the individual's existence is empty. In Zen this state of consciousness is called, "A stone woman who gives birth to a child in the night." In other words, until this realization we are void of all the distinguishing characteristics of our true nature. With the completion of amatsu iwasaka, the human spirit, God becomes self-aware and begins to create. This creation begins with what Lao-tsu called *myo*, the threefold mystery of the divine name. Subjective mind (A U E O) and objective reality (Wa Wu We Wo) are united by the floating bridge of will. Our consciousness becomes vertical (I-Wi), heaven and earth are united, and the child sounds, the thirty-two vibrations underlying all manifestation, are born (see table 4.2). In this way distinctly human consciousness begins.

TABLE 4.2

The Thirty-two Child Sounds

I	Ki	Si	Ti	Ni	Hi	Mi	Yi	Ri	Wi
A	Ka	Sa	Ta	Na	Ha	Ma	Ya	Ra	Wa
U	Ku	Su	Tu	Nu	Hu	Mu	Yu	Ru	Wu
E	Ke	Se	Te	Ne	He	Me	Ye	Re	We
O	Ko	So	To	No	Ho	Mo	Yo	Ro	Wo

Ueshiba-sensei described the kototama in terms of his own experience:

> The kototama is not merely the sound of the human voice. It is the red blood in your hara, boiling over with life. When I chant the sounds of A O U E I, the gods which perform the functions of these kototama gather around me. A true human being can do this and a great deal more.

The soundless sound of the kototama is the cause, not the effect, of vibration. In Sanskrit the primal sound, which creates the form of the universe, is pronounced Aum. It is the manifestation of omnipotent force. In Christianity it is the word *Amen*. In Shinto it is called *Aum no kokyu* and is shown by the lion seated on each side of the entrance *(torii)* of a Shinto shrine (see figure 3.2 in chapter 3).

The lion on the left side of the torii (the viewer's right) has its mouth open, showing infinite expansion (A), the energy of spiritualization (yang). The lion on the torii's right has its mouth closed, showing the manifest world (yin) carrying universal consciousness (Umn). In the words of Ueshiba-sensei,

> The universe begins with the sound of Aaaaa—Ooooo—and its completion is the sound of Umn. The relative (reflected) world manifests the mirror image of heaven, the invisible world of consciousness.

In esoteric Buddhism it is called HAUM—the sixth element, consciousness itself. H is the causeless cause, the originally created; A is first in contrast to all others and therefore is considered as relative being; U is the originally uncreated, the eternal void beyond relativity that knows neither increase nor decrease. AUM is the abbreviated form of A I E O U M N, the constitution of the paradise.

Instinctive mind, the beginning of consciousness, is called *Omou.* O-sensei called it the beginning of the dance of the gods *(kagura mai).* This is known in the Hindu tradition as the primal sound, AUM.

Because language originated in humankind's perception of the kototama, the intuitive wisdom of ancient people can be found in all languages. This wisdom is to be found in abundance in Chinese and Japanese ideograms (figure 4.2).

■ *Figure 4.2: Mikoto: Waves of life energy*

The Japanese word for life is *mikoto,* the same as that for the deity that manifests in human form. Mikoto is the manifestation of *makoto* (true mind). *Ha* is a wave or vibration. *Koto* is "word," but its individual kototama express the meaning "invisible, superspeed, light wave vibration." *Tama* is spirit. In materially oriented civilization, the pure sounds of the kototama become heavy. The sounds of Ko and To become Go and Do. *Koto* becomes *Godo* (or *God*).

Masahisa Goi, the founder of the World Prayer for Peace movement and a close friend of Ueshiba-sensei, wrote in his book *God and Man,* "When *Naobi,* the direct spirit, comes into activity, various high-frequency light wave vibrations are emanated. These create divine spirit and our individual spirit *(bunrei)* as well."[13]

By what light do we view our dreams at night? By the light of life and consciousness. It is the fire that Moses spoke to in the burning bush, the light that has accompanied many other enlightenment experiences recorded in history.[14] Whether we speak of God as light, sound, or life energy, these are all expressions of the kototama, the light of consciousness emanating from the perceiver. Because our perceptions are limited by our senses, we experience light and darkness. In the fourth dimension of pure mind there would be only light.

Each of our senses has a spiritual counterpart. For instance, the sense of sight corresponds to spiritual vision—the light of divine love or compassion. The sense of hearing corresponds to mental stability—intuition and will. The sense of touch is direct connection with nature—instinctive mind (see table 4.3).

TABLE 4.3
Senses in the Fourth Dimension

Electricity (touch)	電	+ mind 心	= 思	instinct, memory
Sound (hearing)	音	+ mind 心	= 意	life-will, intuition
Light (sight)	光	+ mind 心	= 恍	spiritual ecstasy, divine love

The practice of aikido sharpens all the senses and in turn stimulates the growth of their spiritual counterparts. Through aikido training we learn to hear with the mind (intuition), feel with the sensitive ki of instinct, and see through the eyes of compassion. We strengthen our field of ki, thereby elevating both judgment and vitality.

Kototama, the spirit of sound, is the power of life and consciousness. It is the power by which the individual creates his body and enters into this world and also by which the meaning of existence is grasped. The kanji for *sound* reveals the nature and function of this spiritual energy (figure 4.3).

田 Ta—energy field

立 Tatsu—to stand up,
become established

通 Tsu—cycling,
materializing

日 Hi—the sun——————

霊 Fourth dimension
world of spirit

■ *Figure 4.3: Establishing the spirit*

The kanji for "sound" is read as Oм, the Chinese equivalent of Aum. It is composed of the kanji for "establish" or "stand up" *(tatsu),* which refers to the cycling of the electromagnetic field of life, and the kanji for "sun," which also describes the fourth-dimensional world of spirit. The overall meaning is "that which establishes spirit and soul." As our intuitive judgment improves, we are led by our own energy field to become upright in both mind and body. Our posture improves and we gain a sense of morality. The E dimension's judgment rises up to merge with our spiritual origin, the life-will. In yoga this is called the fire of kundalini. The body becomes relaxed and upright and is carried naturally in the hips. In budo, the words for a master of the art are *tatsu jin,* literally, "one who stands up straight." The poet Walt Whitman referred to such a stance as, "Sure as the most certain sure . . . plumb in the uprights, well entretied, braced in the beams. . . . I and this mystery, here we stand."[15]

When we stand up both physically and spiritually, our spiritual (instinctual) control tower, the kototama of Si, becomes activated. Si is the spiritual atom of word consciousness. It is the power of self-realization and all higher intuitive processes. It is absolute (or stopped) speed energy, the hidden deity within the void. This spiritual atom becomes focused and thereby effective through principle (Ri). It manifests as pure reason. Si is expressed as *tsukasatoru,* "to control" or "to take care of." This kototama explains the function of the spiritual atom (see figure 4.4).

With the control tower of Si as stabilizing center, consciousness spirals toward self-realization. An individual may be unaware of the desire to grasp the nature of reality, yet the creative impetus and life-

■ *Oм: Primal sound*

Tsu—pushing strongly;
cycling toward materialization

Ka—adding potential, power

Spiritual

Satoru

Awakening

Sa—difference

Toru—remove, take away

- Figure 4.4: The spiritual atom

- Figure 4.5: Kokoro

force desires to manifest its perfection. As long as body and mind are healthy, it continues to seek new expression. The desire for knowledge is a fourth instinct unique to human beings. It results from the human ability to use the kototama for language.

The first four instincts (desire for food, sex, emotional fulfillment, and knowledge) are like the ebbing of an ocean wave, drawing everything inside. The fifth is intuition, the wave's shoreward surge. It is Ai, the centrifugal energy of creativity, wisdom, and compassion being thrown back upon the beaches of humanity. This is the world of mind, the fourth dimension. It is called *kokoro*.

In figure 4.5, the first stroke (linear) represents innate ability or instinct. The second (plane) is the opening up of self-awareness, the screen on which we create our images. The third and fourth (space and time) represent the interchange between body and mind, subjective and objective consciousness.

The life-will is the fifth dimension, through which all opposition is unified. It is the axis of the kototama principle and is called the *futomani*. *Futo* is the number twenty, the yang (subjective) kototama divided against the yin (objective) kototama. *Mani* is the same as *mana*, the kototama. In religious terms it was called manna. The manna with which Moses fed his people was not unleavened bread but the wisdom of universal order. The Japanese equivalent for manna is mochi, rice cakes. In Japanese mythology we find that in times of difficulty, mochi— abundant wisdom—grew on the trees.

The samurai believed that the misuse of words would rob a man of his youth and vitality. Jesus also claimed, "For by thy words thou shalt be justified, and by thy words thou shalt be condemned." And again,

"It is written that man shall not live by bread alone, but by every word that proceedeth out of the mouth of God."[16]

We can understand the "words from the mouth of God" as universal order or cosmic consciousness. Everything that flows through us, our life itself, is divine love. We utilize this divine energy, putting into effect the wheels of creation for both negative and positive changes. The kototama, however, is whole and complete, and never changes. To the degree that an individual's field of ki conforms to that universal order and perfection, that person is happy, healthy, and wise. O-sensei expressed this as follows:

> If our feeling departs from the love and wisdom of the divine creator, we are not truly practicing aikido.

When human society becomes the mirror image of universal law, an immediate echo to the voice of God, it manifests the constitution of the paradise (see figure 4.6).

Aikido is the experience of human uniqueness. It is a direct intuition, an inductive process within which conceptual understanding must follow the actual experience. Its practice teaches us to be very cautious about basing our understanding, which is always changing, on a one-time experience. We cannot explain well until we have confirmed our experience through years of training.

Once this confirmation has been made, however, we experience a totally new way of relating to our life and our environment. There is a way of thinking that is completely different from that which we have known. It is thinking with the whole body and mind, without preconceived defense mechanisms or plans for success. Finding life's meaning within our own activity we play freely at this serious game. O-sensei stated,

> Man, as a division of the great universal spirit, should already know what it is that he must do.

To create a world of health, happiness, peace, and prosperity is the meaning of human life.

The ancient sages taught that real understanding could be obtained only by the elimination of all dualistic thinking and opposition. "When

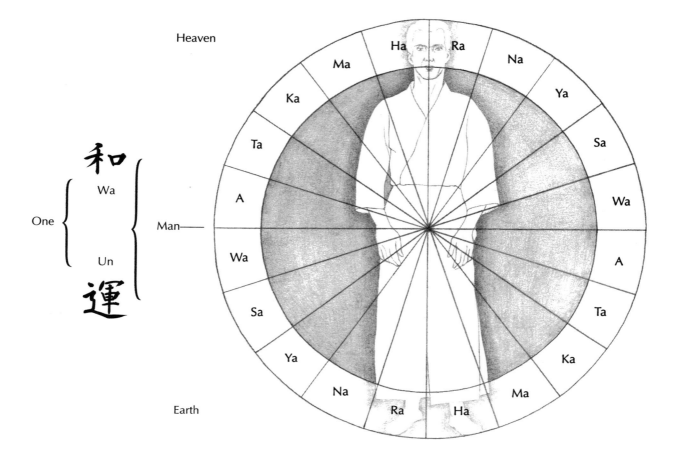

Heaven

One { 和 { Wa } 運 }
Wa
Un

Man —

Earth

Ha   Ra
Ma   Na
Ka   Ya
Ta   Sa
A   Wa
Wa   A
Sa   Ta
Ya   Ka
Na   Ma
Ra   Ha

■ *Figure 4.6: The constitution
of the paradise*

you make the inner as the outer and the above as the below and when
you make the two into one . . . then shall you enter the kingdom."[17]
This kind of intuitive research is the very heart of aikido training. When
there is no longer any difference between the outside (form) and the
inside (feeling) we manifest aiki principle effortlessly.

Humankind is rooted in both heaven (spirit) and earth (body). When
we unite the two through the establishment of vertical consciousness
or spiritual awakening, we move horizontally on the earth and human
society, based on the principle of heaven, is created. This unification
is Wa (peace or harmony) Un (carrying or embodying). It is manifesting
universal harmony on earth.

5 ▪ ONE SPIRIT, FOUR SOULS

▪ *Ichi Rei Shi Kon*

SEEN THROUGH THE EYES OF SHINTO, the vowel dimensions become alive with personality—accessible on the level of human emotion, ideas, and experience. One Spirit, Four Souls is an intricate system of checks and balances enabling us to grow, step by step, in ability and understanding. O-sensei spoke of it in this way:

> *Takemusubi Aiki is the living embodiment and form of the dynamic working of One Spirit, Four Souls, Three Origins, and Eight Powers residing within Taka Ama Hara, the High Heavenly Plain.[1] It is the life-force of the continually unfolding creative energy of universal law. It is you yourself! Man bridges the gap of spirit, mind, and body: the divine, astral, and physical realms. He contains them all. It is his responsibility to protect and nurture them.*

One Spirit, Four Souls corresponds to the five mother sounds of the kototama and together compose the human spiritual constitution (see table 5.1). The *Dai Nippon Shin Ten* explains the four souls as follows:

> Kushitama (I-Gi) expresses the greatest wealth of both heaven and earth and our individual spirit as well. It is therefore symbolized by *heaven*. Aratama (E-Re) gives warmth and heat to the universe and therefore is represented by *fire*. Nigitama (O) is totally flexible and unites all the opposing factors of society and the world. It provides for flexibility within structure (organization) and is therefore represented by *water*. Sakitama (A) brings forth stark reality and the formation or consolidation of the world. It is therefore represented by *earth*.[2]

TABLE 5.1

Shinto Expression of One Spirit, Four Souls

NAME	KOTOTAMA	SHINTO SYMBOL	FUNCTION
Naobi	Su-U	Origin	Reflection
Kushitama	I	Heaven	Intuition
Aratama	E	Fire	Judgment
Nigitama	O	Water	Memory
Sakitama	A	Earth	Spirituality

ONE SPIRIT

The four souls are the function of the One Spirit—*naobi*, both universal spirit and the individual spirit. This is the kototama of Su and U. The cornerstone of aikido is the energy of Su: nonresistance and nonforcefulness—a state of consciousness in which all of our senses are relaxed and at peace, yet completely aware. Smooth, unobstructed movement leads to great power. The central function of naobi is self-reflection: as an intuitive practice, aikido requires constant awareness and assessment of our feelings and intentions.

Naobi is the source of both body and mind. It creates the five senses of sight, hearing, smell, taste, and touch and, therefore, individual existence. As life begins with breath, the ki of naobi manifests in the lungs and the skin. It is the ki of autumn and expresses stark, unadorned reality. The introspection of naobi is not an abstract process of reflecting on the past. It is to stand in the present and see things exactly as they are. Naobi is the virtue of makoto—sincerity and gratitude for the gift of life. A samurai poem states, "Life is a butterfly's dream." Whether we are a butterfly or a human being, we are still the dreamer: the creator of our own reality.

In order to express his understanding of this concept, the Zen master Dogen created an ingenious design of ideograms that may be seen today on the stone handwashing basin *(tsukubai)* at the Ryoanji temple in Japan (see figure 5.1).

The central container that holds the water is a square symbolizing our small or individual self. The circle is our large self, the universal spirit. These are the two sides of *Naobi,* our direct spirit. Engraved on each side of the round stone is an ideogram. These represent the four elements of mind or soul. When each of these ideograms is combined with the square at the center, a new ideogram is formed, expressing Dogen's teaching.

Chinese coins produced around 1004 C.E. were made with a square hole in the center and four ideograms surrounding that hole. The coins, used for fortune-telling, were still in circulation in Japan until recent times, and Dogen, in the thirteenth century, used this form to create the ideogram design for teaching the lesson of self-mastery.

"I only know that I am complete and sufficient just as I am." What sounds like a simple statement here is actually the final stage of the eightfold path to perfect liberation prescribed by the Buddha. The outside circle represents the universal spirit (One Spirit), of which the individual spirit (the square) is a part. The four ideograms represent the four souls: kushitama, aratama, nigitama, and sakitama.

Ware	吾	myself
Tada	唯	just, only
Tariru	足	complete, sufficient
Shireri	知	to know

Another expression of One Spirit, Four Souls is the *gorinhoto* (lit., "the five-level tower of the law"), the five-layer tombstone common throughout the Buddhist world. Its five sections correspond to the five elements of insentient existence (earth, water, fire, wind, and space), which esoteric Buddhism relates to the mind and which Kukai relates to the five primary syllables of the kototama: One Spirit, Four Souls. (One representation of the *gorinhoto* may be seen in figure 7.3 in chapter 7.)

One Spirit, Four Souls composes the river of life. The upper flow A contains imagination, inspiration, and artistic appreciation. If destiny and the construction of human society depend on this realm of consciousness, a great deal of freedom is enjoyed, but we are still unable to establish a high level of civilization. The flow of this ethereal energy is too evasive. It is the deep undercurrent, I, that is the motive power of life, and it is not perceived by our usual consciousness. Its intense energy goes inward and creates sensitivity, intuition, and the highest mental abilities. The flow of this underground river is the most difficult thing for us to grasp, and human civilization therefore cannot easily emerge from this dimension either. The middle flow of the river of life is E U O (reasoning, production, and understanding). It is the realm of human judgment and morality, self-reflection, and intelligence. It is this middle flow that most strongly influences the development of human society.

In Shinto, the human soul is considered to be more than a spiritual aura produced by our body or mind. It is not an abstract existence that h*as* experience; rather, it has no existence prior to experience. It is body-mind, striving to manifest its own perfection. Its healthy function ensures our success and happiness. If we are unable to manifest health, judgment, freedom, and happiness, it is because of an imbalance in One Spirit, Four Souls, the human spiritual constitution.

FOUR SOULS

The unceasing function of One Spirit, Four Souls can be channeled and focused, but it can never be stopped. If any one of the four souls falls out of order, its energy becomes destructive. To counter this, each soul has the ability to highlight the imbalance (the danger); it manifests a checkpoint that helps to override the danger.

Table 5.2 lists the characteristics of the four souls. References will be made to these characteristics in the following discussion of the individual souls.

TABLE 5.2
Characteristics of the Four Souls

SHINTO SYMBOL	SOUL	VIRTUE	MEDIUM	DANGER	CHECKPOINT
Heaven 天	Kushitama 奇	Wisdom 智	Principle 理	Insanity 狂	Satori 覚
Fire 火	Aratama 荒	Courage 勇	Method 法	Quarrel 争	Shame 恥
Water 水	Nigitama 和	Intimacy 親	Amenity 礼	Hatred 憎	Regret/amend 改
Earth 土	Sakitama 幸	Love 愛	Michi 道	Oppose 逆	Fear/awe 恐

奇
魂

■ *Kushitama*

Kushitama: Perfect Wisdom

The virtue of kushitama is perfect wisdom. It remains hidden as the center of consciousness and only expresses itself through the other dimensions. Kushitama's medium is principle: that which allows the balance of dynamic equilibrium and creates effectiveness (Ri). Without its stabilizing function, we are like a wheel without an axle; our own momentum throws us off into insanity.

Perfect wisdom is our true nature, beyond personality and ego. It is not something that we get; it is something that we tend to forget and must constantly practice. It removes all differences and opposition. Inseparable from compassion, it is the checkpoint of kushitama, giving the ability to stand in the center and reconcile all differences. Kushitama, as perfect wisdom, is the power to merge individual will with that of universal order. In the words of Ueshiba-sensei,

> Kushitama, represented by principle (Ri), is the complete manifestation of the virtue of the creator god of Su.

O-sensei referred to it as *ki-musubi*, the tying together of ki, and *ki-tai*, the body of ki; our actual substance. In Shinto it is called "the original concept behind creation."

In the natural world, kushitama is represented in diamonds and precious metals, the essence of the mineral world. It is the power behind birth and growth and unifies the influences we receive from our environment. It creates direct perception, unhindered by emotional judgment. Kushitama gives the individual keen observation, self-control, and the ability to influence others. It creates the most sensitive mental abilities, including extrasensory perception and psychic abilities. At the height of the individual's development, it becomes the power of communicating freely between this world and the invisible world of vibration. If this sensitive antenna malfunctions, the nervous system is affected and we lose contact with reality.

Without the stabilizing energy of kushitama, fire energy (aratama) would burn us out, or water energy (nigitama) would lead us into coldness and withdrawal. Kushitama creates ki from food and sends it upward from the spleen to nourish the lungs and downward from the stomach to nourish the kidneys. It acts as a mediating factor that helps to blend all the other energies, thereby creating a balance of emotions, spontaneity, and fairness. It creates the feeling of total presence and "being there" for others. Kushitama stimulates the nervous system, regulates the birth and growth of cells, and promotes the body's healing power. When this function is overactive, it results in hypersensitivity—we are easily startled—high blood pressure, and neuralgia. To balance this condition it is necessary to stimulate aratama (fire) through physical activity and sweating.

Kushitama's function is the power behind life. When it is deficient, all the body's functions begin to degenerate: the cheeks grow sunken and there is a loss of spirit and vitality. There is a loss of willpower, reasoning ability, and both physical and mental control. Loving feeling and consideration for others declines and one tends to be in the wrong place at the wrong time. Such a person worries constantly; appetites become cravings or no appetite at all; attitudes are artificial. Remedying this situation requires hard work and the nurturing of gratitude. Verbal expressions of gratitude are especially valuable as they resound deeply within us.

Aratama: Control of the Spirit

Aratama, symbolized by fire, creates form and structure. It controls the spirit and creates a joyful and energetic nature. A person in whom this energy is healthy is sensible and possesses courage and the wisdom of morality. Aratama seeks purity and justice and creates a sense of shame when we lack the courage to live up to these ideals. It creates skillfulness in putting ideas into practice. The judgment capacity of aratama leads us to the wisdom of kushitama. A person's level of judgment is shown by the methods used: how everyday problems are tackled, either economically or uneconomically; either according to the principle of natural law, or not. Aratama's nature is a balance between judgment (yin) and courage (yang). If this balance is well established, the person is gentle and kind; if not, quarrelsome, with a humorless sense of superiority. O-sensei described aratama as

> the first function on the earth carrying knowledge and seeking virtue and justice.

Aratama controls consciousness and self-expression. If its energy is excessive, it leads to anger and the heart is damaged. We can lose the

■ *Aratama*

judgment actually to discover the perfect wisdom of kushitama. When aratama becomes weak, support for the will is withdrawn: we become gentle but there is a loss of courage. The will being rooted in the energy of the kidneys, we lose vitality. Finally, the spleen is affected, and the life-force itself is endangered.

The soul of aratama can be destructive. One side of its nature is the harmonizing of opposites; the other side is anger or rage. To avoid this, aratama has the checkpoint of shame or conscience. Persons of high judgment are true to themselves and to others. If aratama becomes weak, we become skilled at procrastination, lose our sense of judgment, and easily tell lies.

Aikido—free from competitive feeling—trains aratama's judgment capacity. Competition does not allow for introspection, and in aikido we must learn to look inside in order to progress. Everyone is susceptible to anger—that very destructive, dangerous emotion. The judgment power of aratama is the catalyst by which we convert anger into humor. O-sensei was known to admonish students harshly at times, yet in the next moment he would be laughing freely and helping them. A person of high judgment never continues anger. To give free rein to aratama in this way destroys the virtue of kushitama.

Aratama is the power of breaking down the old and making way for the new. It governs spiritual purification. When a tree dries up and dies it is from an excess of aratama (sunshine) and a deficiency of nigitama (water) and kushitama (minerals).

Aratama manifests the form of phenomena. In human character it is the spirit of reform and revolution: it causes us to seek justice and truth. Yet if aratama becomes predominant over nigitama, it pushes toward destruction.

Aratama's function creates a healthy, strong metabolism for the elimination of toxins from the body. The training of the physical body strengthens aratama's function, yet if activity is strictly physical we lose balance; the body becomes too thin; thinking becomes diffused; and moral sensitivity is lost. When aratama's function is deficient, the physical body becomes weak; there is a loss of vitality, sexual energy, courage, optimism, creativity, and judgment. In Buddhist terms, the sword of the bodhisattva Manjushri, which severs delusion and establishes justice, is lost.[3]

Nigitama: Beauty in Living

■ *Nigitama*

Among the four souls, the function of leading human society belongs to nigitama. Nigitama creates and preserves the beauty of human life. It creates the gentle power necessary for harmonious unification and reconciliation. It is the main source of our vitality, and when its energy is balanced, the body is beautiful and powerful.

Nigitama must always predominate over aratama. If it does not, orderliness and organization turn into chaos. The virtue of nigitama is intimacy and parental feeling. It is the kototama of O, the energy of gathering, preserving, and connecting. As the main representative of human spirituality, it ties together the highest virtues of human nature: the wisdom of kushitama, the courage and judgment of aratama, its own aspects of beauty and health, and sakitama's love and affection. The word makoto expresses the highest virtue of humanity. O-sensei said:

> Makoto is the interchange or giving back and forth of love. If this
> is lost, nigitama is dead.

Nigitama is the spirit of harmony, materialization, and prosperity. It is the power that makes for good human relations through consideration and amenity. It produces the qualities of greatness: moderation of emotions, magnanimity, a relaxed and flexible state of mind, and both physical and mental power. Nigitama leads with spiritual power and never with force. It is like a deep river, silent and powerful. Its healthy function is necessary for the establishment of world peace and prosperity.

Nigitama's feeling is intimate and self-reflecting. It corresponds to winter, when the leaves fall and life-energy goes deep inside to preserve warmth. If we become overly introverted, however, this ki becomes frozen like ice: we separate from others and lose the flexibility necessary for introspection and harmony.

Nigitama is the first function of naobi—one spirit. As the source of memory, nigitama is essential for making deep personal change. It allows us to feel regret for past actions and feelings and to make amends with ourselves. Nigitama's influence on physical health is reflected in the Japanese term for change, *kui aratameru*, which has the dual meanings of "to change one's attitude" and "to correct one's way of eating."

There is certainly no value in carrying around the baggage of remorse, yet the power to make real change in our lives requires introspection. Real change can never be accomplished by aratama's burning desire alone. The memory power of nigitama must also be deepened until we remember our true nature: only then can real and lasting change occur.

Change is an extremely difficult thing and requires a strong will. Will is the property of kushitama, yet its physical base is created by nigitama—the water energy. If water energy is strong, the will is strong and so is the power to control our own destiny.

Kushitama and sakitama are specialized functions of nigitama. They perfect the two sides of its potential. Sakitama is expansive and elucidates each individual thing, putting it in its proper place; kushitama brings everything together at its own center. This relationship can be seen as follows:

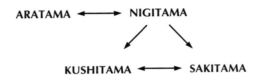

So although kushitama is the motive power of creation, if health deteriorates so also does the power of will. Even though we may regret our past ways, unless we have health and vitality we will most often fail in our attempts at meaningful change.

The word *nigi* of nigitama is from *nigiwau,* to thrive, prosper, or flourish. When this function is well balanced we have abundant health and human feeling. Nigitama is our ancestral spirit. It stores the ki passed down to us from our ancestors. It governs DNA, the genetic code, and the autonomic nervous system. Nigitama determines the length of life. As water energy, nigitama regulates the ki of the kidneys, which store sexual energy and vitality. Postnatal ki from air and food mixes with prenatal ki stored in the kidneys and produces vitality. Nigitama is the root of ki in the body. It produces the yang energy that supports the spleen and also the gentle yin energy that is stored in the kidneys. When water energy runs deep it is silent and powerful, but when it is shallow it becomes noisy, busy, and full of fear.

Nigitama governs the function of ki and manifests the astral body (kitai) into physical form. At birth, nigitama and naobi (the individual's direct spirit) constitute the function of active consciousness. The other three souls are still dormant. In the human body, nigitama supports birth, growth, purification, and regeneration. It presides over the fluids (blood, lymph, sperm, sweat), the hair and skin, the internal organs, and physical health in general. It preserves body heat and immunity against disease. It changes food into nourishment and adjusts the functions necessary for the preservation of health and harmony. Nigitama also determines the health of the bones, the bone marrow, and the brain matter.

Nigitama functions with gentleness while aratama, capable of sudden outbursts, sometimes sacrifices harmony and subtlety to satisfy a sense of justice. When aratama overpowers nigitama, progress becomes an obsession: revolution is considered necessary and there is no listening to others.

Nigitama and aratama are complementary antagonists. Nigitama regulates and adjusts the working of the muscles, takes in nutrition through the process of digestion, and helps to maintain body fluids. Aratama discharges toxins through sweating and the elimination of fluids, changes nutritional energy into physical energy, and promotes misogi through activity. When aratama is too strong, nigitama suffers; and kushitama, as an advanced function of nigitama, is also suppressed. The physiognomy takes on the look of poverty. If nigitama is not overpowered by aratama, the blood is clean and strong; the hair is full and ample, and health in general is robust. When the function of nigitama becomes deficient, generally caused by improper diet, the result is a loss of immunity, digestive power, and the deep memory of our original nature. Such a person becomes attached to smallness and possessions and develops hatred and distrust of others. To cure this situation: adjust the diet; temper the activity of aratama; and nurture a sense of responsibility.

The practice of aikido nurtures both mind and body. It strengthens aratama through physical and mental development and nourishes nigitama through the development of internal ki and health. Aikido practice produces a natural balance between the functions of aratama and nigitama. Those who are overweight lose the excess; those who are underweight put on the needed increase. It helps men to become more masculine and women to become more feminine. Both male and female come into a closer relationship with their essence as human beings.

幸
魂

- *Sakitama*

Sakitama: Manifesting Spirituality

Sakitama, symbolized by earth, creates feelings of love and affection. It also creates a sense of awe and reverence at the wonder of life. In the words of O-sensei:

> The virtue of Sakitama (A) is Michi and this depends on principle (Ri), the realm of kushitama (I). Principle is understood by Sakitama as the key to the flourishment of heaven and earth.

Sakitama is the energy of growth, generation, and development. Its energy goes upward and outward. It distributes ki from the liver to all parts of the body. It produces kindness and patience, tempered with intelligence.

The word *saku* means "to blossom"; *sakaeru* means "to prosper." When this expansive ki is not balanced by control (kushitama) and intimacy (nigitama) it becomes *sakeru* (to break through, tear, rupture) or *sakebu* (to shout). The reverse side of sakitama is *sakarau*, to oppose or go against. It means to go against the natural order of things, to disrupt human progress for small egocentric motives. If we see the small self as the source of power, we become stubborn, forceful, and competitive. To avoid this, sakitama has the checkpoint of reverence or fear. This is not the fear that causes worry or fright, but a sense of awe; a deep respect for life's mystery. This checkpoint directs the energy of sakitama towards michi, the prosperity of mankind.

Michi, the medium or goal of sakitama, translates as path, road, the way of life, or even the divine knowledge of God. Sakitama strives to generate greatness, to create paradise on earth. This is the feeling that creates cathedrals and great cities. It is the nature of people of vision who live and die in service to humanity.

When sakitama is well balanced, it causes us to seek the way of life and manifest it in society. When it is out of order, it produces the nature of a despotic dictator—one who believes himself to be the origin of his own power.

Sakitama's function changes nutritional energy into mental energy. When this function is healthy, we are happy, patient, and have a sense of artistic appreciation. We feel love for people, nature, and God, and often receive moments of intuitive insight. When sakitama is strong, sexual drive is also strong. Such a person seeks a harmonious marriage.

When sakitama's function becomes excessive, so does that of nigitama. When a man and woman become emotionally involved, sakitama's excessive energy stimulates nigitama, resulting in an increase of sexual hormones and body fluids. Nigitama's function of balancing hormones and aratama's function of metabolizing hormones and changing sexual energy into mental energy help to balance the sexual drive. Happiness and prosperity are the result of nurturing the qualities of nigitama and sakitama.

Sakitama governs the emotions. When its function becomes excessive, the result is impulsiveness, anger, violence, or hysteria; such a one is easily stimulated sexually. But if we are unable to give vent to emotions and artistic expression, aratama and sakitama will be damaged. The physical and the emotional are connected; body cannot be separated from feeling. In a happy person, health follows. A person who is full of stubbornness, anger, or selfishness exhausts resistance to sickness.

Sakitama's ki protects us against outside influences; when it is out of order, external stimuli may produce worry, stress, and sometimes craziness. There are two kinds of craziness. The craziness of sakitama is violent, and the person may seem to be going berserk yet at the same time be aware of what is happening. When kushitama is deficient, however, the person is unaware of his own insanity. Sakitama's craziness results from excessive desire; but the real insanity, that of kushitama, is a loss of life-force. When sakitama's function is very deficient, the person becomes as though one of the living dead. There is a total loss of wonder and amazement.

Without sakitama's healthy function, the will to live cannot manifest itself; the liver and intestines become weak, and there is high blood pressure and nearsightedness. To cure the spiritual problem underlying this situation, it is necessary to work for the betterment of society and attempt to help others. Since both sakitama and kushitama are subsidiary functions of nigitama, a total cure must include proper diet.

Sakitama seeks our substance as spirituality. It is that which causes flowers to blossom and buds to come out on the trees. Its energy is strongest in the spring, when thunder rolls in the heavens releasing dynamic tension, the kototama of *goro goro*, and when a gentle spring rain whispers the sound *shito shito*. Sakitama is the dimension of all that is fresh and new, the light of consciousness manifesting the phenomenal world. Nigitama, like the moon, reflects that light and, with aratama, manifests it into form. "And God said let there be light." *Asaaa,* the morning of consciousness.

THE FOUR SOULS IN AIKIDO

O-sensei remained a devout follower of the O-moto kyo branch of Shinto throughout his life. According to the teachings of this sect, when aratama and nigitama are in control it is called the spirit of fire (izu no tama). When sakitama and kushitama lead, it is called the spirit of water (mizu no tama). When the spirit of fire blends perfectly with the spirit of water, fullness and perfection of human and universal spirit are achieved. This is the divine spirit of izu no me no mikoto. O-sensei taught that this was to be realized through the conscientious practice of aikido. Aikido training develops each of the four souls and thereby strengthens the practitioner's spiritual constitution.

Aratama is influenced most immediately through sensitive and precise movements that must be executed instantaneously, without excess or forcefulness. Every technique of aikido is a riddle that must be solved over and over again, each time in a deeper and more sensitive way. In this process we not only strengthen muscles and bones; we also develop intuitive judgment.

Nigitama is most influenced by the development of ki or internal power. This produces health. Internal organs become firm and strong and movement becomes balanced and graceful. We gain confidence and ability and are able to exert a positive influence on those around us.

The development of kushitama comes from studying control and sensitivity. It begins with vertical posture and concentration. In order to master aikido technique, we must develop sensitivity and eliminate the forcefulness that accompanies most martial arts. This leads to stability and natural balance. The study of aikido teaches how to work with the invisible world of ki and how to unify body and mind through kushitama, the life-will.

One of the unique qualities of aikido is its complete openness, both mental and physical. We control the opponent by opening our hands and letting go rather than by holding on and trying to manipulate the other. This feeling develops the all embracing attitude of sakitama,

■ *Figure 5.2: Kannon Sama. Drawing by Taikan Yokoyama (1868–1958).*

beginner's mind. Practice should be approached every day as if it were being experienced for the first time.

In Buddhist art, the peacefulness, wisdom, and control of one who has brought One Spirit, Four Souls into harmonious balance is portrayed as Kannon Sama, the goddess of mercy, sitting serenely upon the back of a dragon (see figure 5.2). The dragon floats lazily, like a cloud in the sky; only the eyes betray restless anxiety, alertness, waiting for the goddess to lose concentration. At that moment, the dragon (the mind and senses) would become a raging beast. Kannon Sama, basking in the light of the moon (truth), has no slackening of awareness, no weak point (*suki*). Truly, the master (will) is at home.

Shinto views the spiritual world as the fire of consciousness. If your soul is pure it passes through you like sunshine on a warm summer day: this is heaven. If your feeling is negative and cloudy it becomes fuel for the fire and you suffer. The spiritual world exists here and now. It is One Spirit, Four Souls. Figure 5.3 shows the complete construction and attributes of One Spirit, Four Souls.

■ *Figure 5.3: Ichi rei shi kon: One Spirit, Four Souls*

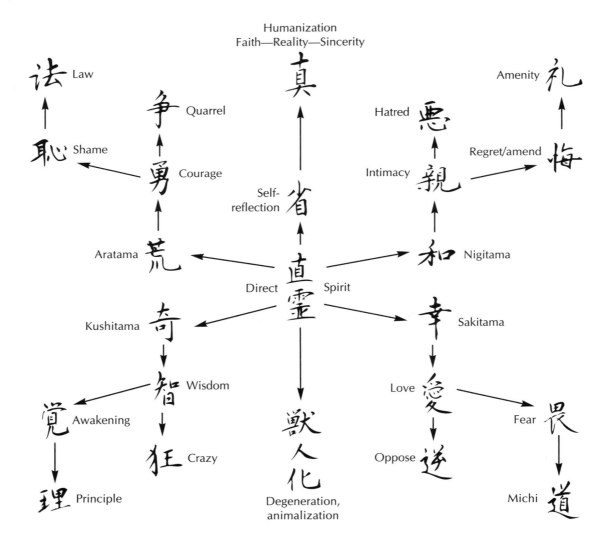

6 ■ THREE ORIGINS, EIGHT POWERS

A CHILD IS AN INDIVIDUAL, DIFFERENT FROM both mother and father yet containing them both. The three are born simultaneously: there is no mother or father until the birth of the first child. Male and female (yang and yin) cannot begin to unite until they have a common bond that comprises both negative and positive. This is the mystery of the trinity. With one we have two; yet two is not two: it is the dynamic threefold function of oneness.

THE THREE ORIGINS

Sangen is the eternal triangle. Known as the Three Origins, sangen is the threefold working of One Spirit, Four Souls, and Eight Powers. In esoteric Buddhism, *sangen* refers to three mysteries. "The three mysteries correspond to the essence, the attributes, and the functions of the Great Sun Buddha, the Dharmakaya Mahavairocana. The three mysteries are the spoken word [sound], visual word [letters], and the reality [kototama] which is realized through meditation. Expressed as the Dharmakaya Buddha, these are so profound and subtle that even the boddhisatvas fail to see them. They are same, different, sameness [asame trisame samaye]."[1]

Sangen is the mystery of *hifumi:* spirit, mind, and body as one, inseparable reality. *Hi* is the inbreath of kokyu; *fu,* or *hu,* is the outbreath. With the inbreath, we fill the body with ki. This is yin, the breath of the earth, physicality, and the power of separation. The outbreath distributes ki throughout the body. It is yang, the breath of heaven, spirituality, and the power of unification. In spiritual practices and martial arts the

■ *Sangen Hachiriki*

outbreath is emphasized. When we receive an attack, we must breathe out and become empty in order to unify with, and thus control, the opponent's ki. The breath follows the mind and with every breath we should unify with the environment. In Buddhism there is the expression, *ichi nen jo butsu*, "One thought moves the entire universe and a buddha is born." In aikido, it is essential to study the role of breath, mind, and ki as one function.

In physical terms, sangen is expressed as fire, water, and soil. For plants to grow, they need sunlight, water, and fertile soil. Similarly, words and thoughts determine spiritual quality, food sustains the body, and the mind is trained through daily activity. Through daily training we experience the joy of vitality, learn to concentrate the mind, and intuitively research the invisible world of ki. Table 6.1 lists a few of these relationships.

TABLE 6.1
Examples of Sangen

Spirit	Sun	Fire	Man	Research	Words	Animal
霊	日	火	人	宛	言	動
Mind	Moon	Water	Woman	Concentration	Action	Vegetable
心	月	水	女	注	行	植
Body	Earth	Soil	Child	Joy	Food	Mineral
体	土	地	子	喜	食	鉱

In Shinto, the Three Origins are referred to as *iku musubi*, the spirit of life; *taru musubi*, the spirit of fullness; and *tamatsume musubi*, the spirit of completion. A traditional Shinto symbol (figure 6.1) portrays the human soul as the three origins, here represented by the three magatama (souls), within a circle (spirit).

The *Dai Nippon Shin Ten*, a very old treatise on the *Kojiki*,[2] describes sangen simply as the essence of the animal, vegetable, and mineral worlds. The symbol for iku musubi, the animal world, is fire. Fire represents the constant birth of life-energy and consciousness. Iku musubi governs the nervous system. It corresponds to the spine (the body's sword) and intuitive judgment. Taru musubi, the essence of the vegetable world, is represented by water. Its nature is flexibility—seeking the path of least resistance and the lowest resting place. Taru musubi represents materialization and change. In the body, it manifests as the circulatory system, blood, and internal organs. It creates relative movement or interchange, the function of creative energy. Tamatsume musubi, the essence of the mineral world—and also of soil—corresponds to the digestive system. Soil represents the basis of physical existence; minerals control and regulate the function of both body and brain. There is no life in the animal and vegetable worlds without the mineral world. Without the trace minerals in blood, the nervous system would immediately malfunction. The minerals in our blood enable us to maintain strength, health, and good judgment. It is said that just as the needle of a compass points north, the iron in our blood enables us to stand up straight and find direction in life.

■ *Figure 6.1: A symbol of the human soul. Photo by Larry Lieberman.*

The imperial teaching in *Kannagara no Michi*, which contains material used in the education of the Japanese emperor, explains sangen in terms of the Eight Powers.[3] These powers (or father sounds) are tendencies toward movement that manifest only when combined with the life-energy of the vowel dimensions (the mother sounds). In the formal study of the kototama *(kototama gaku),* they are expressed through the I dimension as hidden essence. This is called *inochi*, the motive power of life. The Eight Powers manifest as human judgment, and thereby create the quality of human reality, both visible and invisible. They are the foundation of world religion, philosophy, and ancient government. As the properties of the Eight Powers manifest through One Spirit, Four Souls, they create the character of the Three Origins: iku musubi, taru musubi, and tamatsume musubi. The ancient Sanin (Yamakage) sect of Shinto explains: "Kushitama and sakitama are called iku musubi; the power of taru musubi is aratama and nigitama. Tamatsume musubi is a combination of all the souls functioning together."

生立産霊

■ *Iku Musubi*

Iku Musubi, the Spirit of Life and Birth

The imperial teaching mentioned above states that training follows three stages, in which one experiences first iku musubi, then taru musubi, and finally tamatsume musubi.

> Through training we attempt to rise above the dictates of fate and take charge of our own destiny. As yet unaware of our true nature, our judgment is veiled and our training invites constant contradictions. This is the manifestation of Uhijini no Kami (Ti) and Suhiji no Kami (Yi), the first movement of the Eight Powers. The deity Uhijini creates opposition and difficulty while Suhijini creates the stability to weather these difficulties.[4]

Spiritual discipline brings out the difficulties inherent in contradiction and opposition. In this way, the student can realize higher awareness. Just as sickness is the body's attempt to maintain health, without the constant opposition of heaven and earth our planet would abandon its orbit and either fly further into space or plunge into the sun. Similarly, the human spirit does not progress without the contradiction and opposition of the Eight Powers.

Aikido training is both physically and mentally taxing. Physical and mental habits must be broken down in order to rebuild them according to nature's principles. And in this process, *difficulty is our greatest benefactor.* Without it, men and women could never grasp life's significance. It is a great challenge to be strong and yet relaxed; centered yet outgoing; totally aware of oneself yet without vanity or haughtiness.

These contradictions are the product of an internal struggle that must be weathered at any cost. Only those with humility and fortitude will accomplish the path. George Ohsawa stated it as: "The path (Do) is like a furnace that purifies the gold and silver and burns away the other useless materials. There is a rigid physiological selection that eliminates those who do not have the qualities to become masters."[5]

To quote again from the *Kannagara no Michi:*

> Iku musubi is created when the power of contrast comes into contact with the power that creates life and form. In spite of any difficulties, we put forth our utmost effort in an attempt to rise above all obstacles. Yet even as we try to keep a huge and mag-

nanimous feeling, often our hearts and minds become small. Even as we try to overcome chaos and worry, we sometimes become more deeply caught up in them. The harder we attempt to do well, often the more difficult our lives become. We are encountering Tsunugui no Kami (Ki) and Ikugui no Kami (Mi).[6]

Tsunugui creates form and ikugui fills it with life-energy. Through these deities, we gain courage and spiritual stamina, humility and compassion. The interaction between these four deities (Ti Yi Ki Mi) creates the content of iku musubi, the first of the Three Origins.

Taru Musubi, the Spirit of Fullness and Change

Returning again to the *Kannagara no Michi:*

> Continuing our efforts, we begin to sense our spiritual constitution. It manifests as internal power and a feeling of fullness and abundance. Our knowledge and ability grow by leaps and bounds and we feel elated as if there were no limitations on the heights to be reached. Our feeling becomes large and open and we begin to feel that the universe itself is our home. This is the function of Ohotonoji no Kami (Si) and Ohotonobe no Kami (Ri).[7]

■ *Taru Musubi*

Thus, one builds on the other: Ohotonoji produces human consciousness, and Ohotonobe makes that consciousness effective. However,

> Knowledge and prosperity are never sufficient to produce real happiness. . . . Our hearts must be filled with gratitude, peace, and nobility. Continuing still further we begin to manifest the spiritual energy of Omotaru no Kami (Hi) and Ayakashikone no Kami (Ni). The bright light of wisdom and direct perception begins to shine within us and we are amazed at our own happiness. Omotaru provides spiritual power and Ayakashikone embodies that power with a sense of nobility. When you are full of confidence and use that feeling to develop spiritual power, virtue, humility, and compassion, this is the development of taru musubi, the second of the Three Origins.[8]

魂積産霊

■ *Tamatsume Musubi*

Tamatsume Musubi, the Spirit of Completion and Stability

In tamatsume musubi, the final stage of training, we reach the essence of the human spirit, Izanagi no Kami (I) and Izanami no Kami (Wi), the spiritual ancestors of humanity. *Izana* means to unite together with great vitality and joy. Izanagi and Izanami are the very origin of love and wisdom; by the unification of their ki, heaven and earth are united. They are therefore called tamatsume musubi, the power of creation. When the divine love and wisdom of heaven permeates our feeling, the desires of the ego vanish like morning dew with the sunrise. The innate quality of human beings is nothing but goodness and virtue. This is our constitution; our real substance; the invisible background for the stage of life's drama. The source of spiritual light is never defiled.

Through training, the clouds of delusion and negativity are swept away, revealing true nature. There is no end to this process. In the words of Jesus, "Why callest me good? There is none good but one, that is God."[9] We are the imperfect perfection; the sphinx, half way between animal and god. Perfection is not a state to be reached: it is to be found in constant change.

Tamatsume musubi is the completion of sangen. In the words of O-sensei:

> It is the working of tamatsume musubi that creates the mysterious essence of the universe. One Spirit, Four Souls, Three Origins, and Eight Powers functioning in unity establish a vertical center and begin to cycle around it. This creates the spiritual pattern (Hinagata) for the creation of the manifest world.

Buddhism, in Japan, calls the causal body of tamatsume *taizo butsu*. In English, this is the power that creates both body and mind. Using Shinto terms, the exterior form is created by aratama, while the internal organs and ki power come from nigitama. The expansive power of sakitama creates fullness and materialization, and these are all brought together and made functional by kushitama. Through training, the power of will (kushitama) becomes unshakeable and manifests as hara. We are at peace with ourselves and naturally manifest warmth and compassion for others.

Tamatsume musubi is the completion of the human spirit, the eightfold path (Hi Ti Si Ki Mi Ri Yi Ni) of human destiny. This is michi, the kototama of which reveals its true meaning, divine knowledge.

THE EIGHT POWERS

There are many examples of the eightfold progression of michi in Shinto. The following interpretation (see figure 6.2) is told, mythically, as having been passed down from Amaterasu Oh Mi Kami, the twenty-second ruler in the ancient lineage of the sun race, who is worshiped today as the Sun Goddess of Japan.

The chart shows the Eight Powers as a linear progression beginning with the kototama of Ki. Ki stands for research, breaking out of the dark prison of ignorance and studying everything we can find about the meaning of life—leaving no stone unturned in the search for knowledge and truth.

The next step is to refine this knowledge (Mi) and attempt to grasp the principle underlying nature's laws. This demands going inside and becoming intimate with oneself. The result of this searching can be deep spiritual insight and intuition. If we see clearly, the mind becomes an expression of makoto—sincerity and faith (Si). If this true mind is established, decisions are made spontaneously, out of compassion and insight. Such a student becomes humble in the face of the infinite nature of michi, the way. This is true intention (Ni) and it leads the student to seek spiritual training (Ti) in order to go deeper. Through training, we may come to embody wisdom. In this case, wisdom is no longer conceptual and we are able to manifest both power and conviction to create a harmonious and unified environment (Hi). The extension of this power over a wider scope leads—the old texts say—to the ability to bring the country under control through correct government based on spiritual principle (Ri). When this influence extends to the whole world, it becomes world peace (Yi).

Cosmologically, the eightfold path of michi is expressed as the stages of creation. Pure spirit (Hi), meeting with the power of contrast (Ti), polarizes into centrifugal and centripetal force. This trinity (infinity and yin-yang force) manifests as spiritual energy or vibration (Si), which, condensed by centripetal force, creates the world of preatomic particles (Ki) and natural elements (Mi). Natural elements become food for the

■ *Michi: Divine knowledge*

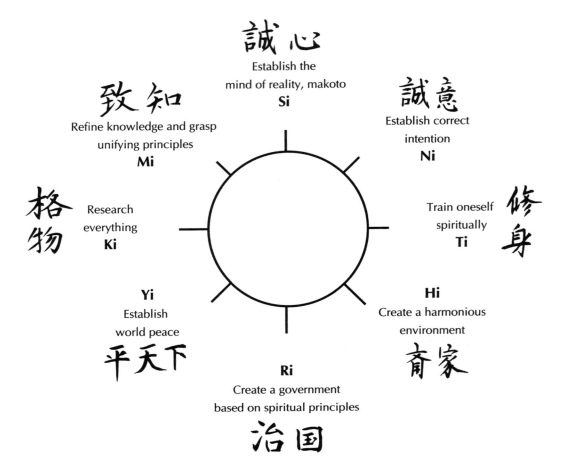

誠心
Establish the
mind of reality, makoto
Si

致知
Refine knowledge and grasp
unifying principles
Mi

誠意
Establish correct
intention
Ni

格物
Research
everything
Ki

Train oneself
spiritually
Ti
修身

Yi
Establish
world peace
平天下

Hi
Create a harmonious
environment
斉家

Ri
Create a government
based on spiritual principles
治国

■ *Figure 6.2: The Eight Powers of Amaterasu Oh Mi Kami*

vegetable kingdom, and the flexible world of spiral forms (Ri) is born. The life potential evolves, in mutual interdependence, in the vegetable kingdom and the animal kingdom, and the life-will reaches upward (Yi) seeking higher forms of expression. Finally we stand up as human beings (Ni).

This progression may also be seen in the evolution of consciousness. The first stage of judgment is immediate mechanical response (Hi): there is no awareness of self or other. This is the judgment of our autonomic nervous system. Second is sensory response—the response to polarity (Ti). At this stage, there is a slight time lapse between stimulus and response. Sensory judgment is followed by emotional sensibilities (Si), with an increase in the time lapse. The response is no longer merely physical and can therefore happen much later. Intellectual judgment (Ki) enables us to perceive abstract reality and manifest it creatively. At this level we tend to see the value of things in terms of our own lifetime.

Social awareness (Mi) leads us to consideration for others and the message of past history becomes important. Ideological judgment (Ri) is very high. Our view is determined by an all-encompassing principle or cosmology. This is the cool judgment of pure reason, which sees time and space as almost infinite.

In the highest stage (Yi) human nature becomes wisdom itself. Standing firmly on the earth with total awareness of his own nature, O-sensei stated,

The universe and myself are one.

There is, however, yet another stage: it is called Bonjin—to be an ordinary person (Ni). Here, no trace of greatness or wisdom remains. In the words of Dogen-zenji, "This traceless enlightenment continues endlessly."

The Trigrams of the Eight Powers

In the O-moto kyo branch of Shinto, the Eight Powers are described as follows:

> All power results from the movement of universal spirit, Ame no Mi Naka Nushi (U). The Eight Powers of movement considered together are called Kokuso Oh Kami, the spirit of fire. They are understood by the descent of Haya Susa no Wo no Mikoto, the spirit of water. Just as the spirit is divided into different dimensions, the Eight Powers of movement are also divided into four complementary pairs. Each of the Eight Powers has its own deity.[10]

Table 6.2 on page 98 illustrates this description.

This translation of the Eight Powers, while providing a convenient classification, is still insufficient as a guideline for aikido practice. The Eight Powers described simply as a balance between opposites (right and left; back and front; up and down; inside and outside) lend themselves better as a reference for our actual practice. Yet this, too, lacks integration with the most fundamental aspects of aikido such as musubi, spiral form, and the generation of ki.

TABLE 6.2
The Eight Powers of O-moto Kyo

POWER	DEITY	IDEOGRAM
Movement	Ohotonoji no Kami	動
Rest	Ohotonobe no Kami	静
Push outward	Uhijine no Kami	解
Stabilize	Suhijine no Kami	凝
Extend	Tsunuguhi no Kami	弛
Pull inward	Ikuguhi no Kami	引
Unify	Omotaru no Kami	合
Separate	Ayakashikone no Kami	分

In order to explain further, it is helpful to see the Eight Powers through the teaching of the *I-Ching*, the book of Taoist philosophy. The basis of the *I-Ching* is a collection of trigrams attributed to the Chinese sage Fu-hsi (circa 3000 B.C.E.). However, these trigrams are also found in the ancient Takeuchi documents of Shinto and probably originated before Fu-Hsi's time.

According to Shinto mythology, during the second generation of the imperial lineage of Japan (before recorded history), fifteen princes and one princess were sent out into the world to educate people in the spiritual principle of the kototama. Just as Japan's symbol of spirit, the sun, shines outward in all directions, they were sent out in "sixteen directions" (i.e., everywhere) to give spiritual light to people. Thus came into being a symbol portraying sixteen branches. It would later become the chrysanthemum crest of the Japanese emperor (see figure 6.3). This symbol has been found in such auspicious places as on the cane and shoes of the Egyptian pharoah Tutankhamen and on the east gate of King Herod's castle in Jerusalem.

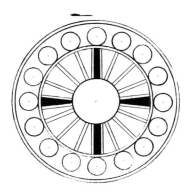

■ *Figure 6.3: Sixteen branches. From the teachings of the Mahikari Kyo sect of Shinto, in Tokyo.*

The sixteen mythic envoys became the leaders of nations, and in the case of some they were deified. They taught the principle of the kototama in symbolic form and—so the story goes—these teachings became the foundations of ancient philosophy and religion.

The princess, Akahitomeso, who went to Mesopotamia, was unhappy to leave her homeland, so her father composed a poem to help her give up her attachment. The poem ("Iroha") is often attributed to Kukai, but it seems to have originated well before his time. It uses each sound only once and is said to be the origin of the Japanese (kana) syllabary. There are many hidden meanings in this poem and it has been intensively studied by both historians and scholars of Buddhism. Every Japanese child still learns this poem as their alphabet.

> *Iro Ha Ni He Ho Ti Ri Nu Ru Wo*
> *Wa Ga Yo Tare Zo Tsune Naramu*
> *U Wi No Oku Yama Ke Fu Koete*
> *Asa ki Yume Mi Si We Hi Mo Sezu*

> You are like a beautiful flower
>   with petals falling down;
> In this world all is constantly changing;
> Today you must cross over the deep mountains of
>   transitory things;
> Dream a sweet dream of life without
>   attachment.[11]

The secret principle of the kototama itself was kept in the East, and the reality of One Spirit, Four Souls, as the dimensions of the universe, is still unknown outside esoteric Eastern religion.

The Chinese interpreted this teaching philosophically; One Spirit,

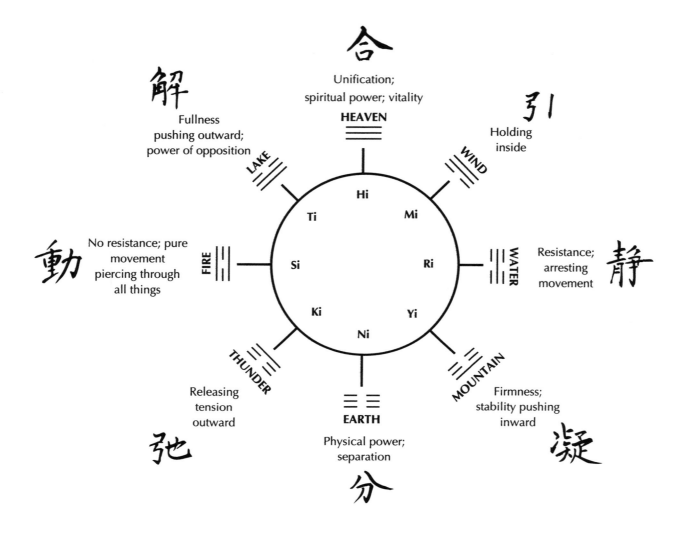

合
Unification;
spiritual power; vitality
HEAVEN

解
Fullness
pushing outward;
power of opposition
LAKE

引
Holding
inside
WIND

Hi

Ti   Mi

動
No resistance; pure
movement
piercing through
all things
FIRE

Si   Ri

静
Resistance;
arresting
movement
WATER

Ki   Yi

Ni

THUNDER
Releasing
tension
outward
弛

EARTH
Physical power;
separation
分

MOUNTAIN
Firmness;
stability pushing
inward
凝

■ *Figure 6.4: The I-Ching and Shinto*

Four Souls became the five elements, the foundation of Chinese medicine and philosophy; and Three Origins, Eight Powers became the basis of the I-Ching.

The trigram arrangement credited to Fu-hsi expresses the a priori universe as an abstract principle of pure polarity. More than a millennium after Fu-hsi, King Wen adopted the trigrams to a temporal order that could be used for divination—he arranged the trigrams in a cyclic order making them susceptible to terrestrial changes and seasonal conditions. In this arrangement, each trigram can be seen as proceeding into another, an arrangement that facilitates explanation of the trigrams yet tends to obscure their quality as polar opposites. As potential energy, the Eight Powers have no beginning or end. They exist only here and now, in nakaima (i.e., in a state in which the absolute and the relative are one).

THE EIGHT POWERS IN AIKIDO PRACTICE

Heaven and earth (Hi-Ni) are pure polarity, the opposite ends of Ame no Uki Hashi, the floating bridge of heaven. Heaven, the creative (Omotaru no Kami), is the power of unification. It is universal kokyu, the source of endless creative power and vitality. "He battles in the sign of the creative."[12] When we realize this deity through actual practice we do not become tired regardless of how much we exert ourselves. The more energy we put forth, the more new and fresh ki we receive. Within this infinite source of ki energy the principle of polarity (yin-yang) works to create the manifest world, our physical body (earth). In aikido, heaven also corresponds to nage, the person who executes the technique.

The receptive, earth (Ni), is the power of carrying spiritual energy. It is the physical body as a division of universal spirit. In aikido, it is uke, the person who receives nage's power ("He causes them to serve one another in the sign of the receptive").[13] Earth is represented by the deity Ayakashikone no Kami, who exemplifies humility, benevolence, and nobility. This is the feeling of a free person. Beyond both greatness and smallness, she carries the universe as her own body and mind. In Lama Govinda's words, "Individuality [Ni] pursued to the fullness of its possibilities is universality [Hi]."[14] Together, heaven and earth represent the origin of human spirituality and nobility. Zen master Taisen Deshimaru told his students, "You should look like a king of lions, always free and strong. If people should happen to see your posture, you should radiate so much dignity that they cannot come too close."[15]

Heaven and earth give birth to three different aspects of movement: power, principle, and form. In aikido, the *power* comes from contrast and stability, the full-body contact of tai atari. The *principle* manifests as spiral movement. The *form* is the product of musubi, which ties one's ki to that of one's partner. Each of these aspects has two components.

Power
Aikido power is like a serene mountain lake. It reflects wisdom and the fullness of spiritual energy, expanding outward with great power ("He gives them joy in the sign of the joyous").[16] Ti is the first movement of mind within hara and manifests externally as power (*chikara*, lit., from spirit).

Aikido's tai atari is not a mere physical collision; it is a complete unification of ki with that of one's partner. In order to practice conflict resolution we need, first of all, an honest confrontation. Ti is yang energy pushing outward and dissolving the hardness and rigidity that binds us. Yi is the power of stability—in aikido, immovability *(fudoshin)*. Like a mountain rooted to the earth and reaching upward, heaven and earth are vertically united by the man or woman who stands between them ("He brings them to perfection in the sign of keeping still").[17]

Principle
The creative light of pure spirit reacting with matter produces the first spark of expanding consciousness ("He causes creatures to perceive each other in the sign of the clinging").[18] Si (fire) is unobstructed movement passing effortlessly through all difficulties. When this feeling meets with our partner's resistance (Ri, water), spiral form is created ("He toils in the sign of the abysmal").[19] These are the powers of spiritual insight and higher reason. Ri is called "the principle that makes movement effective"; Si and Ri, free movement and resistance (arresting movement), create the spiral principle of *takemusu aiki*, spontaneous creation and freedom of movement. In order to utilize this principle, however, one must be free of the egocentric desire to manipulate one's partner. One must have faith in the hara and learn from the partner's movement rather than interrupt it.

The deities Tsunuguhi no Kami and Ikuguhi no Kami (Ki and Mi) are the powers that manifest ki energy as form. These deities correspond to the symbols of thunder and wind (releasing and containing energy). Ki, thunder, engages the wheels of creation. It releases tension through the extension of ki ("God comes forth in the sign of the arousing").[20] Ki is like a sword reaching outward and cutting through all obstructions. In aikido,

• *Chikara*

• *Ri*

it is a handblade cutting effortlessly through the partner's resistance.

This dynamic outburst of energy is brought together by the gentle, magnetic wind of Mi, which creates and preserves life as it envelops and draws energy inside ("He brings all things to completion in the sign of the gentle").[21] Wind is often misinterpreted as centrifugal energy scattering things about: actually, it is inner motion, the power of electromagnetism drawing inward and holding.

■ *Katachi*

Form

In aikido, the functions of Ki and Mi combined create musubi, the uniting of yin and yang. When we tie our ki together with that of our partner and maintain tai atari, our feeling "rides" on our partner's intention as expressed through physical movement. By maintaining correct feeling, the correct form of technique occurs naturally. Our open hands extend outward, connecting with our partner, yet the spiraling of our arms brings him closer, into our sphere of influence. Ki is dynamic power attaching our partner's feeling and initiating movement; Mi encompasses that energy and, like a magnet, holds it inside.

O-sensei taught:

> When aikido techniques of purification are put into practice, the laws of heaven, fire, water, and earth, become understood automatically. The real budo is the way of banyu aigo: *universal love, compassion, and a spirit of protection for all things. Just as your blood flows through and unifies your body, so you must become one with the divine mind of the creator. Michi is to actually train yourself in this consciousness.*

The *Dai Nippon Shin Ten* elucidates this still further:

> First of all you must understand and practice principle, law (method), and harmonious action. Through principle, the correct way of doing things (law) is understood. Manifesting natural law in our daily life, harmony and freedom ensue. Only when this has been accomplished is it possible to practice michi, the way of life.
>
> The one who would understand michi must first understand the body. This requires high judgment and an intuitive grasp of nature's laws and principle.[22]

Michi itself is not a matter of attainment. One who is truly "on the path" is indistinguishable from others yet intimate with all things.

Aikido is an extremely simple form of martial art: it contains only the necessities of self-defense. This simplicity allows the student to concentrate on depth and develop the spiritual aspects of training. The techniques or form of aikido cannot and should not ever be standardized, yet it is essential that the principles of practice be standardized. O-sensei left a map showing the correct way of studying aikido. That map is One Spirit, Four Souls, Three Origins, and Eight Powers.

The Eight Powers may be applied to the spiritual aspect of aikido training: the attitude, or mental stance, necessary to grasp aikido. It is, in fact, these spiritual aspects that must be present if aikido is to be truly understood as michi, a way of life. Figure 6.5 shows the spiritual counterparts of the Eight Powers.

Aikido must always be practiced with vitality (Hi). It should never be broken down into intellectual understanding or fragments of technique. It requires a sense of reality beyond that of brute force. The spiritual power developed through aikido practice can be beneficial or detrimental. It depends on our orientation. Physical vitality must always be tempered by humility (Ni) or it can become arrogance and haughtiness.

The centerpost of aikido is control, and control begins with self-control. In order to maintain a high sense of reality while trying to generate great power, we must maintain a humble and unassuming attitude. If we become arrogant and lacking in concern for others, aikido cannot be practiced safely. If we lose beginner's mind, regardless of our level of expertise, then progress stops.

Aikido is essentially intuitive. In practice, one must develop an intuitive sensitivity to the partner on the outside (ki) and to one's own source of power and centeredness within (mi).

Spiritual practice involves a great deal of repetition. Inherent in this is the danger of falling into the drowsiness of habitual movement. If this happens, regardless of one's physical vitality, practice is lifeless. Always to keep practice vital and alive requires a constant spirit of research (ki). The basic techniques of aikido should be used to research aiki principle from a continually changing and new perspective. Dropping physical rigidity and extending ki throughout the body, the hands

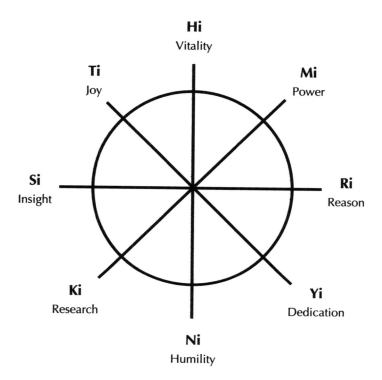

Hi
Vitality

Ti
Joy

Mi
Power

Si
Insight

Ri
Reason

Ki
Research

Yi
Dedication

Ni
Humility

■ *Figure 6.5: Aiki spirit*

become sensitive antennae through which to research the energy world.

Aikido may seem to be magical, yet it is based on natural law. It is completely reasonable and logical (Ri), yet it can be grasped only by developing the ability of direct insight (Si), "seeing" the reality behind form. In order to resolve the apparent contradiction, we should distinguish, from the beginning, things that are possible from things that are unreasonable. The Japanese word for *unreasonable* is *muri*, (lit., no principle). Seeking a method of practice that is reasonable for one's own physical and spiritual condition, one's use of time and effort becomes economical and progress moves smoothly. Reason and intuition should support each other.

The same thing is true concerning dedication (Yi) and joy (Ti). Aikido requires years of dedicated study and training, yet if practice becomes goal orientated it lacks joyfulness and the spirit of aiki is missing. In such a case, no amount of practice will be enough, and it would probably be better not to practice at all. To quote O-sensei again:

Aikido must elucidate the order of the universe, the path towards spiritual understanding. It must always be based on the Eight Powers (the floating bridge of heaven). If this quality is lost it is no longer aikido. Man, as the divided spirit of the universe, must devote himself to the creation of a better world. We must establish a mirror image of the heavenly kototama on this earth. One's individual practice of aikido is a barometer of this activity.

O-sensei borrowed the Buddhist symbols of the triangle, the circle, and the square (figure 6.6) to express the spiritual content of aikido movement. The triangle represents birth and productivity, expansion and separation; the circle represents change and growth; and the square represents fullness and completion, control and solidification.

The triangle. The form of the triangle shows one infinity (Su-U) dividing into relativity (A-Wa). The master swordsman (I) stands within the void of present existence (U) and, shouting the ki-ai IE, his double-edged sword reaches out and divides the heavens and the earth without creating any separation at all. In this way, within infinite oneness subjectivity and objectivity begin. The stability of the kototama of Yi allows the fullness of universal ki to expand as contrast and oppostion, the kototama of Ti. The kototama of Ki releases this abundantly overflowing energy as power and Mi holds it together. Together, they create form and movement. This is iku musubi, the power of birth.

The circle. The forward movement of the triangle creates cycling and interchange—circular or spiral movement. The father rhythms of Si and Ri work within the E and O dimensions, creating abundance and spiritual prosperity. In aikido, this becomes the principle of *takemusubi*, the spontaneous creation of new form (technique). The triangle (entering) and the circle (turning) together create spiral movement, the principle of *irimi-tenkan*. As Morihiro Saito writes in *Traditional Aikido*,

Aikido is generally believed to represent circular movements. Contrary to such belief, however, aikido, in its true form, is a fierce art piercing straight through the center of opposition *(irimi)*. You are not supposed to open your body up widely in an attempt to adapt to your partner's movement but rather to gradually turn the hips *(tenkan)* allowing yourself to continually enter deeper and pass directly through the center of the movement.[23]

The square. The square represents bringing together all of the basic (a priori) kototama of amatsu iwasaka. This is the completion of the human spirit, naobi. The Four Souls unite with the Eight Powers and the human spirit is realized as the constitution of the paradise—tamatsume musubi, the source of wisdom and compassion.

Aikido training leads us through the Three Origins. The triangle represents the spiritual essence of aikido: *masakatsu,* winning directly. This is the spirit of fire: rising up and controlling your partner's attack before it even begins. In ancient budo it is *ko no sen,* "moving first after your partner moves." Accomplished properly, the martial aspect of aikido is over before technique begins. If it is not accomplished, the technique itself, represented by the circle, harmonizing with your partner's energy, cannot even begin. To be able swiftly and skillfully to bring your partner down, however, is not yet mastery: like cutting in swordsmanship, although extremely difficult in itself it is not the totality. Practice is not concerned merely with winning. To carry out the technique into beautiful and harmonious form leads to study of oneself and eventually to mastery, *agatsu.* The person who is only interested in martial ability is still a beginner. It is not enough to be sharp like the triangle: we must remove the edges and become rounded. The student needs firm conviction; the will to grasp her own essence.

The interaction between fire and water creates the final result, earth. In the initial movement of aikido, Ai is already there, yet we can't see it. Only after years of practice does the real content of *ikkyo,* the first teaching, become apparent. More than a linear progression, makatsu, agatsu, and katsu hayabi are all different aspects of the same mind. O-sensei taught that when the triangle, the circle, and the square are combined, they create the symbol of the breath of life (iki):

> It is with profound respect that I venture to liken the aikido symbol
> to the rising sun and the imperial crest of the chrysanthemum [see
> figure 6.6].[24]

When the spiritual aspects of the Eight Powers are balanced and working together harmoniously, aiki wisdom, a sense of our true nature as human beings, is born. Understanding oneself can never be accomplished by mindless repetition or the egocentric practice of comparing one's ability or strength with that of others. Instead, it is when the

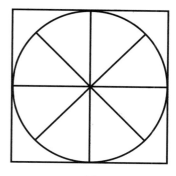

(a)

(b)

■ *Figure 6.6: (a) O-sensei's symbol. From M. Saito,* Traditional Aikido, *vol. 5. (b) Japanese imperial crest. From the Takeuchi documents.*

individual will becomes one with the constitution of nature, the kototama, that real freedom and creativity become possible. Within the emptiness of the great void, all aspects of the manifest world are present. Recognizing them, they become apparent. In Buddhist terms, "Crossing over the floating bridge of the Eight Powers [from Hi to Ni], we are greeted on the other shore *[higan]* by the pure land *[jodo]* of Monju [the bodhisattva of pure wisdom]."[25]

7 ▪ PRACTICE AND PRINCIPLE

WHY IS IT NECESSARY TO PRACTICE SPIRITUAL DISCIPLINE? Why undergo strenuous physical and mental training that to master requires years of dedication? This very question led Dogen, as a young monk studying on Mount Hie, to leave Japan and travel to China in search of the truth. Why, he asked himself, if we already possess Buddha nature, is it necessary to seek it? The Zen story of Nan-yueh and Ma-tsu expresses this koan with typical Zen humor.

Nan-yueh asked Ma-tsu, "What is zazen for?" "I sit to become a buddha," replied Ma-tsu. Nan-yueh then picked up a piece of tile and began to polish it on a rock. Seeing this, Ma-tsu asked, "Master, what are you doing?" "I am polishing a tile to make a mirror!" Nan-yueh replied. "How can you make a mirror by polishing a tile?" Ma-tsu asked. "How can you become a buddha by doing zazen? asked Nan-yueh.[1]

■ *Gyo to Ri*

This is not to say that Nan-yueh was discouraging Ma-tsu from practice; but the message of the koan is clear: we cannot realize anything that is not already a part of us. Ueshiba-sensei expressed it this way:

> *The realization of our true substance and potential is the purpose of creation. The realization of Divine love, the universal consciousness, is our responsibility to the creator.*

To practice aikido is to manifest our natural state; to bring true nature to the surface. Aiki is our innate perfection. It cannot be taught; we must discover it within ourselves. This responsibility cannot be

■ *Dogen zenji*

relinquished to any teacher or path, yet lacking valid training and a teacher's guidance, our potential will never be realized. The search for mastery is an endless process, yet within each moment of practice we should experience the totality of aikido. The end does not justify the means; it *is* the means.

Dogen realized that attainment is our absolute or vertical nature. It has no objective reality, however, unless it manifests through practice on the horizontal plane of time and space. Constant practice, here and now, provides a continual opportunity for true nature to manifest. In the words of the Zen scholar Masâo Abé, "Practice is indispensable as a condition for Buddhahood."[2]

Because technique is a tool for the study of principle, there is no substitute for practice. The student who learns technique more readily than others often overlooks the depth of meaning within that technique. A good attitude, hard work, and self-reflection are the most important factors in learning aikido. The student who cannot gratefully receive criticism progresses slowly; the one who finds and corrects his own mistakes progresses rapidly and in depth.

In *Shobogenzo*, his most important work, Dogen wrote,

> In the great way of the Buddhas and ancestors, surely there is a supreme ceaseless practice which continues endlessly. Through this ceaseless practice sun, moon, and stars move and all things exist. The virtue of ceaseless practice is never hidden, therefore the mind is aroused and practice begins. Its virtue, however, is not immediately revealed and thus it cannot be seen, heard, or comprehended. Although it is not revealed, do not study it as something hidden.[3]

This ceaseless practice is the movement of nature and the universe itself. Even when we sleep the mind never ceases its function of seeking perfection. Within change, the steadfast will constantly seeks to manifest its infinite potential. The Zen phrase, "The master is at home" does not imply *knowing something* but rather a state of *being* that is totally aware.

Modern education and lifestyle train the intellect, yet we are not taught how to direct our basic instincts constructively and fulfill our human potential. We are not given a practical method by which to develop intuition. The problems and illusions created by the conscious and the subconscious mind can be solved only by establishing intimacy with the real self.

Among nature's creations, only mankind covets the illusion of independence from nature's laws. We live in a sheltered environment, yet the human mind is like a dangerous jungle. We spend so much time listening to the mind's abstract monologue that we are closed to a wider or deeper awareness. The emphasis of aikido is not on fighting outside enemies, yet the need for self-defense is always present. Become lazy or complacent and you lose the real battle without ever knowing the enemy: your ego. Lacking self-realization, we are led away by doubts and delusion from our true goals for the sake of momentary whims. This weakens our will and confidence: in the animal kingdom, we would never survive this way. Nature insists on severe training for survival, and modern man seems to have lost sight of this fact.

When we begin to lose our connection with nature, we receive warning signals such as sickness and misfortune. Stagnation leads to disease, fear, and loss of freedom. To remedy this requires purification. The function of the autonomic nervous system is the continual resolution of inner physical conflicts that could otherwise lead to stagnation. However, purification involves accomplishing resolution on a conscious level. This is the object of training: to bring us into harmony with nature on a conscious level. The practice of aikido gives us an awareness of nature's harmony and economy and leads us toward true intimacy with life.

Aikido is the way of harmony. Within love there is severity and power and aikido's nature is not passive. Training, however, is not a matter of torturing the body: unreasonable training injures both body and spirit. As "nature made conscious," training should not be a matter of physical abuse.

Spiritual discipline requires the intensity of a life and death commitment if it is to have deep and lasting value. Just as the cicada sings itself to death in the late summer, each person who would discover their own nature must pursue that reality with every ounce of life within them. Aikido does not teach us to become passive; rather, it teaches us to direct our intensity inward rather than oppose others.

Freedom exists only within structure, and depends on an acute

■ *Figure 7.1: Motogaeri: Returning to the source*

■ *Figure 7.2: The spiritual form of Ru. From Matsuzo Hamamoto,* Bansei Ikkei no Genri to Hanya Shingyo no Nazo *(Tokyo: Kasumigaseki, 1948), 211.*

responsiveness to our environment. Migrating ducks follow perfect formation: the leaders turn and the rest of the flock, too, change their direction. This is not a game of follow the leader. They are in tune with nature and each other. This is aiki—winning without fighting; cutting before the sword is drawn.

Daily practice teaches us to use our animal instincts in a humanistic way. This is an unending growth process and there is no resting place. The perfection of nature lies in a state of impermanence, in constant and instantaneous adjustment. When we are free of the tension, doubt, and illusion that block the natural state, tension is gone from body and mind and we are able to create freely. By furthering that release of tension, aikido fulfills the original goal of religion, *motogaeri*, returning to the source.

The motogaeri symbol (figure 7.1) shows the function of aikido movement: returning to our true nature (Su). The principle of aiki expresses endless unity. A tree, grown from a single seed, extends its trunk and branches and in turn bears fruit that eventually grows another tree; just so, all things must return to their origin. Failure to do so causes waste, chaos, insanity. We are born from our own life-field *(hinagata),* and unless mind and feeling merge with that origin we miss the meaning of life.

Su is pure movement without obstruction. It manifests through its carriage, the kototama of Ru. This is the beginning of vibration, an almost infinitely short-wave vibration passing effortlessly through the material world. It is *katsu hayabi,* instantaneous attainment—neither yin nor yang, movement nor rest, offense nor defense. In the East there is a proverb that states, "In order to travel great distances, the sage rides on the back of the dragon *(ryu)."* This is the kototama of Suru, the nearly infinite-speed energy of cosmic consciousness. The spiritual form of the kototama Ru is shown in figure 7.2.

The unique principle, *muso genri*, governs all movement in nature; it produces the movement and power of the universe. It manifests as the four dimensions of spiral movement. Beginning with the kototama of Su, the ki of fire expands (A) and separates (E), attempting to return to its spiritual origin. This is symbolized by the triangle (figure 7.3). The continuation of this movement creates the sign of the circle; the ki of water contracts (O), energy joins together, and materialization begins. Finally the stabilizing ki of earth (I) becomes established and all the

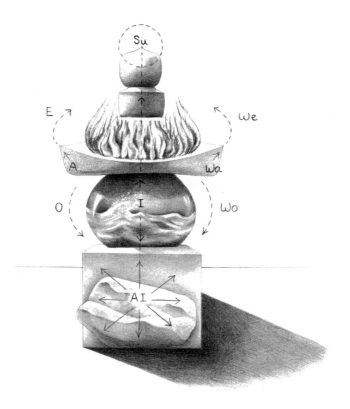

■ *Figure 7.3: Muso genri: The unique principle*

dimensions are unified within the void or U dimension. This is the foundation of Ai, love and wisdom. This creative energy begins from hara, the one point of the kototama of Su. Su is the beginning of *kokyu*, universal breath, movement, and power.

Studying aiki principle as kokyu, breath and spirit, we manifest the kototama of Su, developing intuition and spontaneous creativity. The expansion/contraction cycle of the breath is the first manifestation of life's principle. Breath is the essence of many spiritual and martial disciplines. Breath, ki, and mind are inseparable and study of the breath leads to an understanding of ki and mind. "The link between body and mind, spirit and posture, attitude and technique, is breathing. In the end, posture and breathing become one."[4]

The word for breath in Japanese is *iki*, "the ki of the will." As a verb, it is *ikiru*, "to live." This is the motive power behind the kototama of Su. Through kushitama, this kototama, spirit, mind, and body are unified. In Shinto this is called hara.

CREATING AN IMAGE

The principle of aikido is most simply explained in this way: All movement begins from the one point of hara (see page 25). In the body this is tanden no ichi, the physical center. Aikido technique begins from the expansion (A) of this point. Unable to extend the arms further, they begin to cycle (E) and create form. This form creates the method through which our natural weight (O) rides on top of our partner's center. The complementary/antagonistic functions of E and O must be continually supported by the expansion of A or we lose connection with Su, pure movement, and the one point (I) of hara. If each of these stages is not supported by its origin, the movement can only be accomplished by unreasonable force.

Developing direct and intuitive insight into aikido requires creating a working image of how aiki principle manifests in practice. This image enables us to see beyond form into the reality of technique. As insight and ability increases, this image will be reevaluated and refined.

Within our one spirit (Su-U), the first movement of kokyu begins to draw inward and the center (I) is established. With the outbreath, spiral form and function (Suru) begins. Suru manifests the first principle of aikido, the absolute and the relative as one function.

Although the body moves as one unified function, each of its parts has its own function and position. In one way of speaking, there is no difference between feeling and form, hara and hands; yet they are not the same.

The first technique of aikido is *ikkyo* (lit., first teaching) (figure 7.4). It manifests the kototama of Suru. More than an isolated technique, ikkyo is the study of immediate control. The technique must be finished the moment we touch our partner, or even before. If you attempt to throw your partner by pushing you will become overextended and vulnerable. This is the most common mistake in the practice of ikkyo. Let your arms rest on your partner by their weight alone, yet transfer your entire body weight to the receiver. Any attempt to bring your partner down by the power of your arms stops their natural function, the creation of form, and your weight cannot rest squarely on your feet. This way you lose verticality, the origin of your power.

How do we manifest the kototama of Su in practice? All movement and power must be an effortless manifestation of hara. When your

■ *Figure 7.4: Ikkyo-suru: Absolute and relative as one movement*

partner makes full body contact, relax and absorb him completely until his energy hits the center of your hara. This center is the one point in the body that remains firm and stable. It is your vertical concentration, and it creates a dynamic tension that unifies your relaxed body. Extending outward and inhaling, fill your body with ki. Exhaling, merge with your partner's ki. This enables you to move your partner as easily as if you were moving only your own body.

The physical training of aikido is, of itself, spiritual training. Practice begins with deep breathing, *shin kokyu* (figure 7.5). The relaxed arms

■ *1*

■ *2*

■ *3*

■ *4*

■ *Figure 7.5: Shin kokyu: Deep breathing. The relaxed arms extend outward, but only enough to facilitate bringing energy into the hara. The inbreath accompanies the opening of one's feeling, and hara acts as a vacuum, drawing the ki of both heaven and earth into the body through arms, legs, and even the pores of the skin. The exhalation is slow and controlled.*

■ 5

■ 6

extend outward, but only enough to facilitate bringing energy into the hara. The inbreath accompanies the opening of one's feeling, and hara acts as a vacuum, drawing the ki of both heaven and earth into the body through arms, legs, and even the pores of the skin. The exhalation is slow and controlled. In aikido technique, the breath is seldom ever discharged forcefully. Even in the case of a shout (ki-ai) accompanying a movement, only a small amount of air should be released from the lungs.

Shin kokyu is the practice of centering and also learning how to "hold" one's mind and ki. Try to feel how the breath makes contact with the inside of your body. It should feel as light and soft as a summer breeze, yet full-bodied. Then duplicate that feeling in the way you make contact with your partner.

In partner practice, the study of kokyu begins with *kokyu ho*—literally, "the way of breathing" (figure 7.6). This is the most basic training of musubi, tying your ki together with that of your partner. It is practiced in *seiza*, that is, sitting formally on your knees, with your partner firmly holding both of your wrists.

Kokyu ho is a study in the essence of *ma-ai*, time-space relationships. Although it seems that your body and that of your partner are in full contact, there is still space between skin and bone. This space is mind

呼
吸

■ *Kokyu: Breathing*

■ 1

■ 2

■ 3

■ 4

■ Figure 7.6: Kokyu ho: The way of expansion and
contraction. In kokyu ho it is essential to absorb
your partner's power completely so that it
becomes useless against you.

■ 5

■ 6

itself. Do not attempt merely to push your partner over. It is essential to let the partner come into your sphere of influence if you want to unify with him and control him. If you use your kokyu to absorb his power and redirect it appropriately, you will control him effortlessly.

The kototama of Aum (mentioned in earlier chapters) is manifested in *Aum no kokyu*, the opening and closing of the cosmic mudra (see figure 7.7). *Aum no kokyu* shows one of aikido's basic movements.

The U dimension, the most balanced, begins as Su, pure, unobstructed movement. This is the spiral form of kokyu ho and ikkyo. Through *tenkan* (pivoting) Su opens up as A. AE disperses the energy upward through the creation of form and O sinks downward, creating the power of hara. Finally we return to the voice of Umn.

In partner practice, this becomes *kokyu osae* (figure 7.8). The power of the O dimension's capacity is most emphasized in osae techniques, where the partner is brought down slowly, rather than thrown.

Throughout the entire movement, the stability and control of the I dimension, the motive power behind Su, remains hidden, yet this dimension is the sensitive antenna that makes the other dimensions

effective. Holding everything together through dynamic tension, the vertical plane—rising, sinking, and turning—creates power and control and makes technique effective. This vertical concentration is the source of our power. It must never manifest directly, however, but only through the horizontal turning of the hips. Rising upward, this force creates intuition; sinking downward, it creates vitality.

■ *Figure 7.7: AUM no kokyu: Opening and closing the cosmic mudra*

A Zen koan asks: "Standing on top of a one-hundred-foot pole, how do you take a step forward?" Throughout practice, we continually reach new plateaus and confront the difficulty of taking yet another step into the unknown. If you attach to your present state, however advanced it may be, you are stuck; progress stops.

Remaining centered, relaxed, and naturally upright while dealing with your partner's attack, learn the correct mind and feeling for going beyond this problem. This is the mind of *inori*—the mind that unites heaven and earth through your own body. It is the principle (Ri) of the will (I). It means to ride *(nori)* on the will. In Japanese, the kototama of *inori* means "prayer."

Aikido is a form of moving prayer. Through activity, it brings all the aspects of spirit and soul into harmony and efficiency. When mind originates in the hara, posture naturally becomes straight. The left (spiritual) and right (physical) sides of our body are united in dynamic movement and we learn to ride on the waves of our partner's will.

The power and form of inori is shown in figure 7.9 as a sword movement that O-sensei created from Shinto purification rites. Standing firmly in the center, the sword of judgment spirals upward, connecting heaven and earth.

In swordsmanship, this connection is shown in the movement *kurai dachi* (figure 7.10). The kanji for kurai is written as man (亻) standing (立). It also means "the number-one position," the vertical connection between heaven and earth. Kurai dachi adapts ame no hashi date (figure 7.9), or inori, to partner practice. The sword *(tachi* or *dachi)* must be used as part of your own body. In kurai dachi you must draw the power to penetrate your partner's defense from your vertical posture. Ikkyo is the barehanded form of kurai dachi.

With a slight variation in timing, the basic kurai dachi movement becomes the advanced form of kasumi (figure 7.11). A fog or mist obscures uketachi's (the person who receives the sword attack) view and until the last moment he thinks he has won. You must lead him to commit himself totally.

In kurai dachi and kasumi, as in all the movements of aikido, it is necessary to move directly into the attack in such a way that a collision seems inevitable. The collision is avoided, first by unifying with the partner through kokyu, and second by *irimi-tenkan* (entering-pivoting).

Tenkan is somewhat like the Taoist symbol for yin and yang. Uke,

I
Will

Nori
Ride upon

▪ *Inori: Prayer*

▪ *Yin and yang*

- 1
- 2
- 3
- 4

- *Figure 7.8: Kokyu osae: Bringing your partner down by control. You must not attempt to push down on or break through your partner's resistance. Rather, let the extension of your arms (A) lead him out of his hara. In this way your natural weight (O) will bring him down easily.*

■ 5

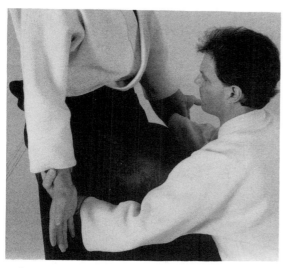

■ 6

the receiver, and nage, the one who throws, are like two magatama, continually changing position and function. The attacker becomes the one who is thrown and both sides completely change positions.

In aikido, however, the circle is not only two-dimensional rotation: it also travels a larger arc of forward movement. Tenkan is always combined with irimi as one principle. As ability increases, the sphere of one's forward movement becomes so large as to appear, in the short space of forward movement, to be a straight line. The greater the radius of this sphere, the greater your control and ability.

■ *1*

■ *2*

■ *3*

■ *4*

■ *Figure 7.10: Kurai dachi. Rather than pushing on your partner's sword, you must draw your power from your vertical concentration and make direct hara-to-hara contact with him.*

■ 5

■ 6

Consider how the solar system travels the spiral path of the Milky Way galaxy even as the planets circle the sun. Similarly, your partner must travel around your forward movement: you are the sun; your partner is the earth; and the mind that connects you with your partner is the moon. Just as the moon moves the tides of the earth, nage must control uke's body by controlling his mind or ki. To the degree that you radiate reality (sunshine) to uke, it will be passed to him as correctness and truth (moonlight).

Irimi nage (figure 7.12) manifests the kototama of iku musubi, Su-A, the opening up of spiral motion. On a vertical plane, it is the rising and descending spirals of izanagi no kami (I) and izanami no kami (Wi). Irimi nage is an example of up-down, right-left, back-front, and inside-outside (ame no uki hashi) as one unified and balanced movement. Whichever participant breaks the sensitive connection between two partners, that partner becomes immediately vulnerable to attack.

Irimi (entering) is made possible by tenkan. But this does not happen by trying to avoid or get around your partner. Your hand, properly resting on the top of uke's spine, and your body weight riding *(inori)* on his physical center of balance together accomplish the dual purpose of leading him away from his center and bringing him down by his own

■ *Kurai dachi*

■ 1

■ 2

■ 3

■ 4

■ Figure 7.11: Kasumi: Mist. Any
attempt to sneak under your
partner's sword will end in failure
and he will strike you. You must
enter directly into his attack and,
with an imperceptible difference in
timing, arrive at his right side.

■ 5

momentum. You should not interrupt his direction of movement. Use it fully. In order to control your partner, you must blend perfectly with his movement and feeling. You have to learn how to *see* your partner correctly.

The method of entering irimi is shown with short sword *(wakazashi)* against long sword (tachi) in figure 7.13. Leading ukemi to the opposite side of your entrance, your feeling must pass under his arm rather than going around his body. Trying to avoid his sword you will be hit. It is said that the difference between success (life) and failure (death) should be as thin as a sheet of paper.

Neither the verticality of kushitama nor the flexibility, grace, and beauty of nigitama must be sacrificed in order to accomplish technique. The study of aikido through nigitama is the study of communication. Nigitama (sinking) and aratama (rising) create the relative movement of the technique (taru musubi—the circle). Neither can function effectively without the other.

The movement of the solar system exemplifies aiki principle. The centrifugal force of earth tries to fly the planet off into the realms of infinite space; at the same time, the centripetality created by infinite expansion (heaven's force) balances this, and thus is earth confined to cycling peacefully within its orbit around the sun. This same principle exists in the spiral form of irimi nage (figure 7.14).

This is universal kokyu. When we practice deep breathing (shin kokyu) we extend ki out to infinity (A), and will (I) sinks deeply into the hara. When we intuitively grasp this simultaneous centripetal and centrifugal function (Ai), we find meditative stillness within activity. "Should you find true immobility, there is immobility within activity."[5] Actually they are the same thing. In aikido, the body must be completely relaxed, while the mind should maintain a 360° awareness and be intensely focused on our situation.

Ten chi nage, the heaven-earth throw, exemplifies the basic principles of kokyu (figure 7.15). Within the U dimension, movement and stillness as one, you establish your center (I) and feeling opens up, creating form (Ae) as body sinks downward (Oum) creating power.

The square is the symbol of control and stability; of wisdom and compassion. In *The Art of War*, Sun-tsu said: "The greatest success is to win by apparent defeat." So, too, the fastest way to develop in aikido

■ 1

■ 2

■ 3

■ 4

■ *Figure 7.12: Irimi nage: Entering throw. Irimi (entering) is made possible by tenkan. But this does not happen by trying to avoid or get around your partner. Your hand, properly resting on the top of uke's spine, and your body weight riding (inori) on his physical center of balance together accomplish the dual purpose of leading him away from his center and bringing him down by his own momentum. You should not interrupt his direction of movement. Use it fully.*

■ 5

■ 6

■ 7

■ 8

■ 9

■ 10

■ 11

■ 1

■ 2

■ 3

■ 4

■ *Figure 7.13: Irimi with short sword. Leading ukemi to the opposite side of your entrance, your feeling must pass under his arm rather than going around his body. Trying to avoid his sword you will be hit. It is said that the difference between success (life) and failure (death) should be as thin as a sheet of paper.*

■ 5

■ 6

■ 7

■ 8

is to eliminate the attitude of competition. Control and consideration are the ingredients that create real power and ability.

The most difficult part of any technique is the beginning. If you are able to reach the advantageous position of throwing at the end, you should bring your partner down with a controlled and expansive motion. In this way, preserve and develop the power of kokyu and also avoid opening up a suki, or weak point. It is anticlimactic to attempt to throw your partner with great force when you have already put him in a weak position.

UNIFYING ONE'S KI FIELD

In order to manifest the power of aikido, the body must move as a unit. All its parts must be synchronized like the workings of a fine watch. Extension of ki is not just the extension of the arms. It is *ki wo haru* or *kibare*, the extension of ki in all directions and from every part of the body. Maximum extension occurs with arms slightly bent. The ki of the hara connects directly to the elbows and then to the wrists and the fingers. Each part is connected like a string of pearls. The shoulders should be held back and down, with the chest open. The shoulders, wrists, and all the joints of the body must be able to move freely. If the wrist is tight, for example, it will cause stiffness in the elbow and then the shoulder. Tightness in any one part of the body leads to tension throughout. When your body is flexible, mental control is possible: merely by adjusting the wrists and the direction of your fingers, you can blend your ki with your partner's feeling.

In the basic hanmi stance of aikido, the hands turn slightly upward as if holding a sword in the seigan stance. At the same time, ki is sent downward from the wrists. With a slight adjustment of the hands, adjust the focus of your mind and blend with the uke's movement. This body-mind coordination is the original method of yoga. It is similar to the effect of a beam of light shining through a prism: the entire spectrum of light branches out. The light is consciousness *(mikotoha)* or life-force (ki). The prism is sangen—entering, unifying, and controlling as one function. O-sensei taught:

■ *Kibare: Ki extension*

> *Enter in the sign of the triangle, perform the movement (tai-sabaki)*
> *of the technique as a circle, and control or bring down in the sign*
> *of the square.*

Enter in the sign of the triangle is the first teaching (ikkyo). It has three aspects: (1) entering directly and immediately controlling your partner; (2) immediately offsetting your partner's balance; and (3) immediately changing his mind so that he has no intention of continuing to attack. The circle adds the aspect of tenkan to irimi and is best studied through the irimi-nage technique. The circle represents change, establishing ki-musubi and completely changing positions with your partner. The square is best studied through the shiho nage technique. O-sensei stated that

> *Shiho nage is the basis of all kokyu nage techniques.*

Studying shiho nage leads to final stabilization of the hips: hara becomes truly centered and the power of kokyu is intuitively understood. The square represents control. When the triangle, the circle, and the square become united, the Eight Powers of human judgment manifest correct technique and form.

■ *Figure 7.15: Ten chi nage: The heaven-earth throw. Within the U dimension, movement and stillness as one, you establish your center (I) and feeling opens up, creating form (Ae) as body sinks downward (Oum) creating power.*

■ *5*

■ *6*

■ *7*

■ *8*

■ *9*

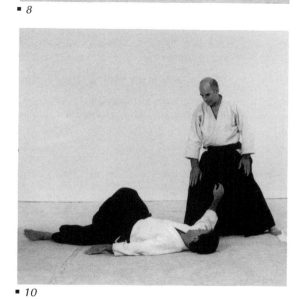

■ *10*

■ *1*

■ *2*

■ *3*

■ *4*

■ *Figure 7.16: Tegatana: Handblade. Consciousness of the handblade in all our techniques is the key to unifying our arms with the power of hara. The blade (little finger) connects the ki of our arms to our hips. It must always cut through to uke's center.*

■ 5

■ 6

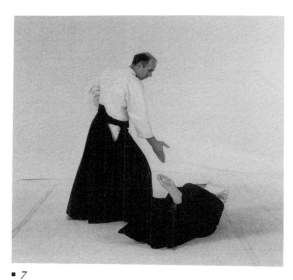

■ 7

In aikido the hand is used as a blade. It is called a *tegatana,* which means "handblade." When this blade is placed on our partner's body, we seek the path of least resistance. Executed dynamically, these hand movements—which should have the same feeling as actually cutting with a sword—enable us to cut through our partner's resistance and throw him (figure 7.16). Variations on ikkyo show the use of the handblade. The ki-ai of *Ie,* unique to Japanese budo, helps to keep a strong center while cutting outward.

■ 1

■ 2

■ *Figure 7.17: Kesa giri: The basic cut.
In order to manifest the power of hara
through your sword, your concentration
(ki) must go out from the tip of the sword.
Rather than trying to hit uke's sword, your
hara must pass through your own sword
in such a way that your entire body
weight rests on his hara. This exemplifies
the kototama of Aei. The cycling (E) of
your sword results from the inability to
extend (A) any further.*

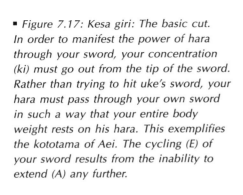

■ 3

■ 4

■ 5

■ 6

■ 7

All aikido techniques utilize the handblade. Not only the form of aikido but its feeling as well can be found in swordsmanship. Every technique of aikido requires cutting—cutting without a sword. Practicing sword is extremely beneficial in grasping aikido's true feeling. The most basic cutting exercise is *kesa giri* (figure 7.17). Practicing this movement daily will eventually reveal many of the secrets of aikido.

In aikido, as in swordsmanship, the true sword is the mind. The swordsman disciplines his mind so that his sword will effortlessly cut through the opponent's opposition. In aikido, however, mind cuts

■ 1

■ 2

■ 3

■ 4

■ *Figure 7.18: Yonkyo: Cutting without a sword.*
Just as in the kesa giri movement, you must not
push on your partner's wrist. Instead, your
concentration (ki) should pass through uke's arm to
his hara. Attempting to do yonkyo by causing pain
to uke's wrist will usually result in loss of control.

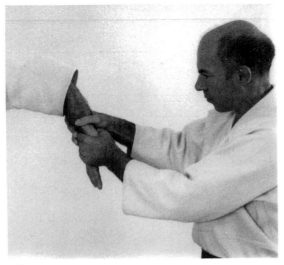

• 5

• 6

• 7

• 8

through the opponent's opposition yet leaves his body completely intact: the principle is the same, but the partner is given life and ki rather than a death blow. This exemplifies the ideal of *katsujinken,* the sword of wisdom that gives life. Cutting without a sword is well illustrated in the *yonkyo* movement (figure 7.18).

If you attempt to manipulate your partner, correct form will be impossible. Holding your partner's arm down with your natural weight alone, his whole body feeling will rise up in an attempt to overthrow you. This is especially well illustrated in figure 7.16. Taking advantage

■ 1

■ 2

■ 3

■ 4

■ *Figure 7.19: Morote tori kokyu nage (jo): Receiving and dispersing your partner's energy. Sinking into the center of the technique, unite with uke. Receive your partner's power in your hara and redirect it through your arms. Through the spirit of aratama (fire—E), the energy of the collision is dispersed upward so that the centripetal power of nigitama (water—O) can bring uke down. These energies are not separate from their source, nor are they independent of each other.*

■ 5   ■ 6

of this, you can enter into his center and accomplish the technique. If, however, you push down on him with the strength of your arms, you will lose control. You must find the point of balance that forces him to protect both the upper and the lower parts of his body.

Maintaining verticality and moving forward, natural weight is converted into power. When you meet your partner's opposition, this power is converted into two functions: (1) centrifugal (fire, E), expressed through the arms as form; and (2) centripetal (water, O) expressed as ki or power (figure 7.19). In aikido, these two forces occur simultaneously. Although physical contact remains on the outside of the partner's resistance, mind, or ki, must penetrate directly through his power and control him from the inside.

Sinking into the center of the technique, unite with uke. Receive your partner's power in your hara and redirect it through your arms. Through the spirit of aratama (fire—E), the energy of the collision is dispersed upward so that the centripetal power of nigitama (water—O) can bring uke down. These energies are not separate from their source, nor are they independent of each other.

Aikido technique begins with (tai atari) body contact and expands in spiral movement as musubi, the tying together of your ki with that of your partner. The spiraling of your arms should unfold naturally from

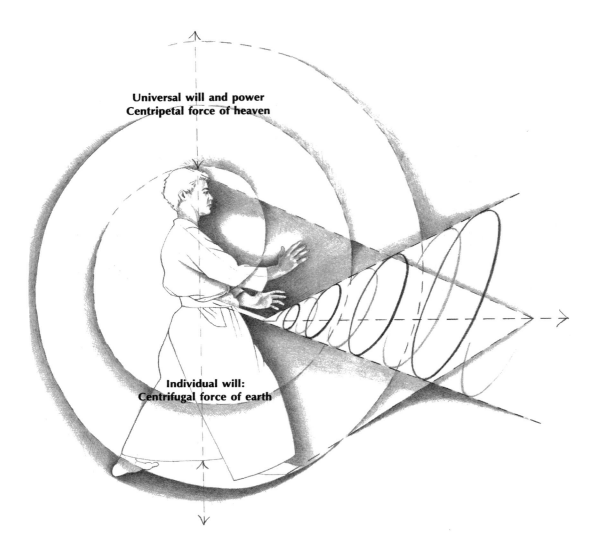

Universal will and power
Centripetal force of heaven

Individual will:
Centrifugal force of earth

■ *Figure 7.20: Hito*

the hara and result in effortless and imperceptible power and control.

Visible form (aratama) appears to be the power of the technique, but its function is to disperse uke's power and thereby avoid a direct collision. The real power (nigitama) is invisible, yet it meets uke directly. He is unable to discover its source, let alone oppose it. When these functions are balanced, you can effortlessly pass through the center of the technique (Su) and bring uke down by weight alone. This is the study of our inherent spiritual power as human beings. In Japanese, the word for a human being is *hito*, which translates as "the fixation of the spirit" (see figure 7.20).

The simultaneous function of aratama (E—rising) and nigitama (O—sinking) is also clearly seen in the movement of kote gaeshi (figure 7.21). The close-up (photo 9) illustrates how uke's energy not only rises as he attempts to recover but also sinks simultaneously as he falls.

In figure 7.22 this simultaneity is again shown in morote tori kokyu nage (ge). Here, *ge* simply denotes throwing downward, as opposed to *jo* (upward) in morote tori kokyu nage (jo).

In figure 7.23 we see katate tori kokyu nage (jo). In jo techniques we offset our partner's balance downward. His resistance to falling makes it easy to throw him upward. In ge techniques this principle is reversed. In either case the two tendencies must be part of one movement rather than an action-reaction sequence. The form of the hand is a lotus flower (photo 4). The little finger stands up almost straight and is the center of the hand's spiral form.

In order to control your partner's body, you must control the space that unites you. The katate tori forms of ikkyo and kokyu nage (figures 7.24 and 7.25) show the method of controlling inside and outside simultaneously.

Large and total body movement is the best way to discover the power of hara, yet unless you maintain honest body contact (tai atari) you become vulnerable. Just as the sun shines on the earth at all times, nage's focus must always enter directly into ukemi's center. The *seigan* stance of swordsmanship (figure 7.26) indicates the correct way of seeing the partner. In the ancient martial arts, this one-pointed concentration *(kime)* was used to thrust *(tsuki)* with a sword or spear, or to deliver a blow to the enemy's weak point. O-sensei taught:

All techniques begin with the thrust.

This kind of focus is a point within a circle, the symbol of Su (figure 7.26).

In barehanded techniques *(taijutsu),* this central focus expands into the periphery, creating spiral or circular form. This is shown in figure 7.27 in the omote form of ikkyo. Photo 3 shows a point within a circle *(maruten),* the principle of seigan in movement.

The sword form sode suri (figure 7.28) uses this same circular form to enter directly into a shomen uchi attack from a gedan stance. Photo 3 shows the way of entering to the left without giving your intention away to your partner.

■ 1

■ 2

■ 3

■ 4

■ *Figure 7.21: Kote gaeshi: Returning the wrist throw. Kote gaeshi requires an extremely subtle connection and can never be successful merely by twisting or causing pain to uke's wrist. You must offset his balance before he can recover to attack you. Photo 9 illustrates how uke's energy rises (E) as he attempts to recover and sinks (O) simultaneously as he falls.*

■ 5

■ 6

■ 7

■ 8

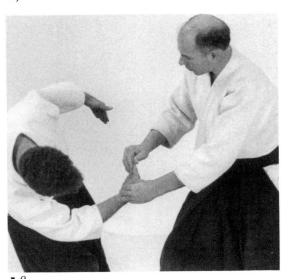

■ 9

■ 10

■ *1*

■ *2*

■ *3*

■ *4*

■ *Figure 7.22: Morote tori kokyu nage (ge). In order to throw kokyu nage downward (ge) you must send his energy slightly upward, letting your forward movement and the sinking power of your hips offset his balance. If you raise your arm, however, uke will escape. Merely indicate the direction of your concentration with your fingertips. The correct turning of the handblade is also necessary to break through the power of both of his arms.*

■ 5

■ 6

■ 7

■ 8

The ideal of aikido is to balance time, space, and position:

> *When my partner attacks, my sword is already resting at his throat*
> *or I've already cut him from behind.*

These words of O-sensei were also expressed as *katsu hayabi,* moving with the speed of the gods. There is no action-reaction here, only moving together harmoniously. In order to accomplish this oneness, there can be no thought of winning or losing, no separation between

■ 1

■ 2

■ 3

■ 4

■ *Figure 7.23: Katate tori kokyu nage (jo). Katate kokyu nage exemplifies the movement of thrusting with a spear. In barehanded technique the hand becomes like a lotus flower (photo 4), the little finger standing up nearly straight as the center of the hand's spiral form. This kokyu nage clearly shows how the mind must be directed by the direction of the fingers.*

■ *5*

■ *6*

■ *7*

■ *8*

self and other—in other words, no ego. Moves like mikiri (figure 7.29) help to develop this feeling of oneness. In mikiri, the uchitachi (the attacker) takes the initiative (sente), cutting the vision of the receiver before he can counter.

Balanced techniques can be performed on one foot. Ikkyo on one foot (figure 7.30) illustrates the one-pointed balance of the Eight Powers of aikido. This ikkyo is used when it is dangerous to take even one step backward.

■ 1

■ 2

■ 3

■ 4

■ Figure 7.24: Katate tori ikkyo: Inside and outside. If you push against uke's arm you will be stopped. The teaching here is that you must send your energy out of your fingers and down into the earth. In this way the power of your hara can penetrate to uke's center. This teaching is also the key to dealing with kata tori techniques. Do not attempt to lift uke's arm except by the raising up of your entire body.

■ 5

■ 6

■ 7

■ 8

Koshi nage, performed from a nikkyo position (figure 7.31), is another example of the one-pointedness of aikido balance. This move is impossible unless one's mind is well rooted in the hara.

All power is the result of being intimately connected with nature. With movement this power begins to manifest. In a black-belt seminar in 1975, Yamaguchi Seigo-sensei said,

> Tai atari doesn't mean recklessly colliding with your partner's body, yet if you collide with ki, your partner will go flying as if

■ 1

■ 2

■ 3

■ 4

■ Figure 7.25: Katate tori kokyu
nage: The control of space. This
kokyu nage shows how to control
the inside and the outside of the
technique simultaneously. Katate tori
techniques are the most fundamental
practice of musubi (tying your ki
together with that of uke).

■ 5

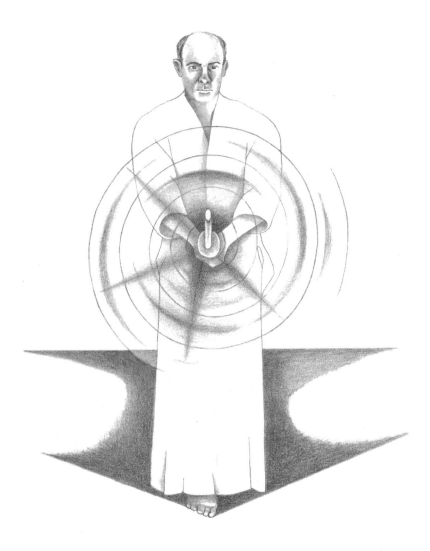

■ *Figure 7.26: Seigan gamae: Ready to thrust. Seigan literally means "the correct way of seeing." Your concentration must control uke's center and also encompass his form completely.*

picked up by a large wind. To acheive this, your mental energy *[ki]* must be centered in your hara. Your entire body must be flexible and yet immoveable. It must be strong and vitally alive. The legs and feet must be stable and firmly planted without faltering, yet able to move freely. I remember the image of O-sensei: wearing traditional cloth socks *[tabi],* yet moving with lightning speed across the mat, never faltering, like a mountain but without hardness. It seems that above and beyond being a genius of budo, his total awareness of his own existence naturally gave birth to the divine techniques *[kamiwaza]* of aikido.

■ 1

■ 2

■ 3

■ 4

■ *Figure 7.27: Ikkyo omote: A point within a circle.*
This is the principle of seigan (figure 7.26) in
movement. It is a point within a circle. The central
focus expands into the periphery, creating spiral form.

■ 5

■ 6

■ 7

Natural movement is more than correct biomechanics. Aikido movement occurs from deep inside, from our life-force. The muscles of the body are relaxed, yet there is a state of dynamic tension existing within our feeling.

Seeking understanding through the physical experience of repetition builds a strong body and improves technique. But you will never fully grasp aiki principle this way. Attempting to manifest technique according to your ideal of what it ought to be develops knowledge, yet is insufficient. A new way of learning must be found: using the body to research feeling, intuition, power, subtlety.

■ 1

■ 2

■ 3

■ 4

■ Figure 7.28: Sode suri: Sword spiral. Sode suri means "sliding on your partner's sleeve." It uses the spiral form of ikkyo omote (figure 7.27) to enter directly into a shomen uchi attack from a gedan stance. Photo 3 shows the way of entering to the left without giving away your intention.

■ 5

■ 6

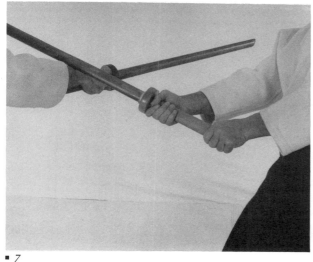

■ 7

■ 8

■ 9

■ 10

■ *1*

■ *2*

■ *3*

■ *4*

■ *Figure 7.29: Mikiri: Cutting the vision. The ideal of aikido
is to balance space, time, and position.*

*When my partner attacks, my sword is already resting
at his throat or I've already cut him from behind.*

O-sensei called this katsu hayabi, *moving with the speed of
the gods. There is no action-reaction here, no thought of
winning or losing, in other words, no ego. This is* ko no
sen, *moving first after your partner moves.*

160

■ *5*

Training goes through definite stages. At the first or second dan level, we understand the movement of basic technique but are still troubled with the problem of combining flexibility and power. Training fluctuates between the practical and the ideal. Attempting to be strong, we become tight or rigid and gracefulness and beauty are lost. Trying to be relaxed and perform more ideal aikido, we become weak and ineffective. Lacking the experience of hara, our approach to aikido is necessarily dualistic.

At the third or fourth dan level, we begin to experience hara and manifest the power of ki over physical muscle. However, we still cannot maintain an even level of calm mind and control regardless of the size or skill of our partner. We bounce back and forth between hara and technique. When we lose hara, we depend on correct technique to lead us back to it.

Finally, through continual effort, hara and technique are synthesized. Faith in yourself allows you to move forward without any planning or strategy. Mind and concentration remain unchanged, regardless of your partner. Such a master can move freely from hara; and technique is born according to necessity. In aikido, this is a master of seven dans or more. And still there is further to go. Feeling and intuitive understanding must be integrated into every aspect of our lives. Aikido is a lifetime of practice and research.

George Ohsawa writes in *The Book of Judo*:

> Aikido constitutes a principle underlying all religion, philosophy and science and it can, therefore, help to solve the ideological problems of the world. Through practical movements which require judgment, reasoning, and instant action, it teaches respect for others, the superiority of softness and adaptability over strength and unreasonableness, and a view of life based on harmony and natural order.[6]

When the triangle, the circle, and the square become one harmonious function, this is suru, the spiral working of the human spiritual constitution. This was understood in ancient times as suberu, a model for governing the people. The ancient name for the Japanese emperor was Sumera no Mikoto. The word *sumera* comes from *suberu*. It means to

■ *Suberu*

■ *1*

■ *2*

■ *3*

■ *4*

■ *Figure 7.30: Ikkyo: No retreat. Aikido techniques always maintain one-pointed balance. This is a physical expression of ame no uki hashi. Standing on one foot, our verticality is reinforced and we become even more stable than standing on both feet.*

■ 5

■ 6

■ 7

govern according to the wisdom of One Spirit, Four Souls, Three Origins, and Eight Powers, that is, to use only the slight amount of effort necessary to bring the wheels of creation into motion—a momentary appearance of our spiritual substance. In Zen, this amount of effort is "to raise even one speck of dust." It is—to use a political metaphor— to govern in such a way that everything goes so smoothly that people do not know there is any government: they feel that they accomplish everything by their own efforts and the leaders sit back and watch

- 1

- 2

- 3

- 4

■ *Figure 7.31: Koshi nage: One-pointed throw. Balancing on one foot, the weight of uke's body makes us even more stable and roots our consciousness strongly in our hara.*

■ 5

■ 6

■ 7

contentedly. This is possible only when there is government by sages, where the objective of the leaders is only to deepen their understanding of universal law and use it to lead people toward health, harmony, and spiritual enlightenment.

8 ■ THE ORDER OF THE UNIVERSE

■ *Uchu no Chitsujo*

AIKIDO IS THE STUDY OF NATURE'S LAWS and the universal principle underlying them. The basis of natural law, as of every individual's existence, is the principle of change, or movement. Aikido technique manifests this principle, yet in order to produce a healthy and harmonious society, this ability must also become a part of daily life.

Although appearances are constantly changing, all things are united through aiki principle. There is no separation between spirit, mind, and body; the physical and the spiritual. Nature is the product of universal breath (kokyu), centripetal and centrifugal force. The infinite universe is the periphery of the body. The individual physical being and the environment are one inseparable continuum, each being food for the other.

If we desire to live simply, free of excess, nurturing a closeness with nature and universal law, we should understand that taking care of this world and taking care of ourselves are inseparable. As the basis of humankind's existence is physical and spiritual food, food is also the fundamental mechanism of change. Taking care of body and mind begins with an awareness of the fundemental importance of food. This has been stated since ancient times: "Food is the chief of all things. It is therefore said to be medicine for all diseases of the body. From food are born all beings, which being born, grow by food. All beings feed upon food, and when they die, food feeds upon them."[1]

Everything we take into the body is a kind of food. The higher vibrations that feed intuition are spiritual food. The elements—fire, earth, air, and water—create the vegetable world, our physical food. Within each level of manifestation is the seed of the next. Through eating, we communicate with the environment. Controlling the activity of one's mouth (eating and speaking) is taking responsibility for one's life.

In Zen Buddhism it is said, "A day without work is a day without food." This is not merely glorifying the value of work as a sacred activity: a meal taken without working becomes excess in our body and makes our ki sluggish. This is especially so in the case of animal food, which is much harder to digest than grains and vegetables. All things in nature have their own spirit or electromagnetic field. In addition to physical nutrients, food also supplies us with ki energy. Michio Kushi writes: "The nourishment we receive from food depends primarily on its ki, or quality of natural electromagnetic vibration, not on its physical characteristics such as amount of calories, protein, vitamins, or other nutrients."[2]

Creation takes place from the infinite void: the U dimension. Pure spirit (Su-U) creates polarity (A-Wa), the ki of fire and water (yin and yang), and aiki principle is born as the vibration of life. A single movement of mind, "one particle of dust," and the world of vibration begins. It is the individual's first food and creates the ki-body and pure intuition. The O dimension condenses these vibrations into the world of pre-atomic particles. This state creates the physical elements, which in turn produce the vegetable and animal worlds; the life-will then manifests as human life. In the Upanishads it is written: "The lord of beings meditated and produced prana, the primal energy, and rayi, the giver of form. . . . Food is prana [ki] and rayi. From food is produced seed, and from seed, in turn, are born all creatures."[3]

Human intuitive judgment and instinct are the right and the left hands of God, the world of pure a priori spirit. Intelligence comes from the vibrations of the pre-atomic world. Our bodies—in our blood— contain the oceans. Solid organs are the continents and the tissues holding them together are the roots of trees and other vegetation. The lungs are two great trees; and the intestinal villi, through which human beings digest their food, are the ancient grasses and seaweeds that grew beneath the primeval oceans. The billions of bacteria in the body are the tiny animals living within the earth. In the earth, they create food for the vegetable world; in the human body they facilitate digestion. Nature is destructive to human beings only when its natural order and balance are disturbed.

Society is built on the idea that yang (man, forcefulness, science, modern) is superior to yin (woman, gentility, tradition, ancient). History reconciles the destruction of (yin) primitive people through superior weapons of force (yang). Science (yang) is used as a tool to conquer nature (yin) until the earth, upon which our life depends, is endangered. In an effort to cleanse itself, the earth is in revolt. Will human beings be discarded as little more than a symptom of nature's illness?

That is the macro situation: a similar micro process is occuring in our bodies. Hara, the human physical center of balance, is located in the center of the small intestine. It is a production place for both physical and spiritual energy. If the digestive system is weak, physical vitality, as well as spiritual potential, declines. When the intestine is weak, posture slumps forward and the spiritual control tower (kushitama) begins to topple. "If we are unable even to defend ourselves against tiny microbes and bacteria, how can we possibly expect to do so against an enemy with malicious intent."[4]

Taking care of our own health is the first step of self-defense. If we want to realize the principle of aiki in daily life, we should first put our bodies and minds into harmony with nature. The person who truly understands her own nature can never blame others, or her environment, for sickness or misfortune. Living under the illusion of separation, we become defensive and forceful. We blame our environment for the maladies created by imbalance in our own lifestyle. Yet the cause of all problems is only our way of thinking.

Human beings have the capacity to realize the nature of their infinite origin. From birth we begin to return to our origin through the expansion of consciousness. We eat more and more from the world of higher vibrations and ki.

The evolution of human beings is based on the laws of nature. Human form and abilities have traditionally been based on a diet of mainly grains and vegetables. We have thirty-two teeth: twenty are for chewing grains, eight are for cutting vegetables, and four are for tearing meat. This 5–2–1 ratio suggests that cereal grains have been the principal human food since prehistoric times. In the East, rice has always been respected and even worshiped as a source of both physical and spiritual vitality. At the center of the ideogram for ki is written the ideogram for rice. The ideogram for rice illustrates the Eight Powers of the life-will, the I dimension.

With the beginning of the industrial revolution, Western dietary habits began to lose the orderliness of tradition. Today, much food—

■ Ki: Life energy

even outside the West—is chemically produced, chemically preserved, and prepared without an awareness of natural balance. No longer relying on whole grains as the staple, much of the world's population is losing physical and spiritual fortitude—hara, or center. Many look for short cuts to understanding.

In order to acheive the high goals of aikido, health and vitality are essential. This begins with proper food choices. The human constitution at birth is largely determined by the mother's diet and activity. To be born with a strong, healthy body is a wonderful gift: the potential for self-development is almost unlimited. Regardless of pre- and perinatal influences, however, for many people it is when they begin to choose their own food that freedom as an individual begins. As we grow more distant from parental influence, we begin to recreate a constitution in accordance with our own spiritual quality.

You can put aikido into your daily life, not by keeping your mind always focused on your one point, but by using aiki principle in all that you do. That begins with taking charge of your own life and destiny. You are not likely to change everything in your environment to suit your taste absolutely, but you can control how you perceive your surroundings—and controlling your perception changes everything. Using aiki in your daily life requires makoto, a sincere and honest approach.

Through the practice of aikido we grow, day by day, mentally, physically, and spiritually; we develop the power of ki or *kokyu ryoku* (breath power). This strengthens the immune system—indeed, the entire constitution. It is even possible that it changes the structure of DNA.[5] Through training, we attempt to discover inner strength and flexibility: firm on the inside and flexible on the outside. This maxim is based on Chinese military strategy:

> *The one who is flexible on the outside and strong*
> *on the inside will continually flourish.*
> *The one who is strong on the outside and weak*
> *on the inside will flourish momentarily.*
> *The one who is flexible on the outside and weak*
> *on the inside will lose what he has.*
> *The one who is strong on the outside and hard*
> *on the inside will inevitably be destroyed.*[6]

To be flexible on the outside and strong on the inside is the ideal constitution. People who are weak on the inside and strong on the outside may experience some limited success, yet unless they can reverse their constitution, their happiness will be short lived. The person who appears gentle may have much more internal power than the one who looks powerful. Real power manifests as health, suppleness, thoughtfulness, and a deeply reflective personality. These qualities exemplify the constitution of an aikido master.

In the beginning of training, most people are hard and rigid on the outside—like an egg: brittle on the surface and soft at the center. Through training, we generate life-energy (ki) and become increasingly firm and strong inside. Finally, that exterior defense system shatters and we become peaceful and happy.

Ki is the basis of human life. It is the reality of mind and controls the breath. When breathing is disorderly and uncontrolled, mind and ki are unsettled. Breath should be long, deep, and fill every part of the body with vital energy. It was said in ancient times that a samurai crossing a long bridge would breathe only three times.

Extremes, in quality or quantity of food, hinder the process of training. O-sensei's humorous statement,

If you think practicing aikido is hard work, try eating all morning

is more than jest. An excessive quantity of food weakens ki and makes it sluggish. In a healthy state, the blood is slightly alkaline. When ki becomes sluggish, the blood becomes acidic, and we begin to lose physiological adaptability. This eventually leads to physical sickness. Large muscles decrease the flow of ki in our body and result in a loss of sensitivity. An overweight person lacks stamina and is soon out of breath. When you stop your breath, your ki stops and your muscles tighten. You lose contact with your spiritual essence, the sound of Su.

Animals instinctively know what and how much to eat. Cows eat only grass, yet they produce enough protein to build huge bodies. Wolves eat few vegetables or fruits yet they produce vitamin C in their own bodies. This kind of adaptability insures their well-being and the evolution of the species.

Humanity, in its exalted position as the spiritual leader of the animal kingdom, has yet to mature and come into its own. We are like a newborn monarch, an heir apparent, as yet unaware of our duties as the ruler of the domain. We easily override our instincts and succumb to pleasure or convenience, eventually undermining our own adaptability. Unless this situation is corrected we eventually lose aiki, the ability to transform chaos, conflict, or difficulty into harmony.

Ueshiba-sensei taught:

> *The creation of a better world begins with the purification (misogi) of our physical organs (rokkon shojo).*

This physical, or metabolic, aspect of misogi (aratama), must also be balanced by nigitama's discharge of ego delusions and sense of competitiveness. This is mitama migaki, the polishing of spirit and soul.

Mitama migaki is the complement of misogi and is, in effect, the polishing of intuitive judgment. Higher judgment reduces the necessity for hard physical practice. One's movement becomes more economical and effortless. An older person cannot continually put forth the same amount of physical effort as a young man, yet O-sensei practiced until his final days. He hardly touched his attackers. His power was not that of physical muscle: it came from a deep understanding of his own being and the Do (Tao).

Morihei Ueshiba endured great difficulties and soul searching. He exhausted every means within his scope of knowledge to improve himself. Not only was his daily practice relentless, he also refined himself through religious studies, poetry, and the daily chanting of Shinto prayers. After the age of fifty he became completely vegetarian. He preferred his wife's simple cooking to lavish food.

Ueshiba-sensei expressed the highest level of aikido as michi: every part of daily life as training. During his intensive training sessions (gasshuku), his main staple was often simple unpolished rice. He taught that aikido and agriculture are parts of one path and encouraged his students to grow their own food. In 1950 George Ohsawa wrote in *The Art of Peace*: "For eight years Master Ueshiba has been living in a very simple cabin on a hill in the countryside, two hours north of Tokyo by train. He lives there with several of his disciples. He cultivates his fields alone following the Japanese tradition. Last year he harvested 640 kilograms of rice; 800 kilograms of potatoes; several hundred kilograms of red (azuki) beans, some wheat, buckwheat, and some vegetables."[7]

■ *Mitama migaki*

■ *Sakurazawa Yukikazu:*
George Ohsawa

Sakurazawa Yukikazu, who in the West is known by the name George Ohsawa, was a close friend of Ueshiba-sensei. He wrote over two hundred books on the ancient cosmology of the Far East and played an important part in introducing the essence of Far Eastern philosophy and medicine to the West. He helped to introduce aikido to the West by inviting Minoru Mochizuki-sensei to Europe in 1951. In *The Art of Peace* he expressed his deep respect for O-sensei and aikido:

> For a master of aikido or judo to die in an accident, or by sickness before the age of seventy, is unlikely. This person's physical, physiological, spiritual, sociological, and biological adaptability is healthy and strong. . . . Adaptability, incidently, is based on powers of memory and creative imagination—a kind of ability to foresee the future. If one is to become a master *[shihan]* of judo or aikido, one must be able to know beforehand all the various possibilities which might occur within time and space.[8]

Aikido is training of the mind and body, centered and unified by the spirit. The philosophy and medicine taught by George Ohsawa is a physiological and philosophical expression of aiki principle.

O-sensei set down four stages of progress through which we must pass in order to reach mastery. They are compared here with the four stages taught by George Ohsawa (see table 8.1).

TABLE 8.1
The Four Stages of Development

UESHIBA	OHSAWA
l. Power	Health
2. Technique	Judgment
3. Harmony	Freedom
4. Michi	Happiness

The first level (power/health) is self-explanatory. Unless one has a certain degree of physical strength and stamina, true health is lacking.

The second level (technique/judgment) eliminates the need for great strength or forcefulness. Higher judgment is recognized through greater economy of movement and the ability to accomplish more with less effort and in less time. This criterion separates the master of technique from the beginner.

Level three (harmony/freedom) is the ability to move freely in spite of obstacles or resistance. This comes from within; it cannot be given to you, or withheld from you, by anyone but yourself. This is not the lack of conflict, but rather its constant resolution in harmony. (Lack of conflict would be the end of life itself: if such a condition were possible, the sun would shine constantly and no food would grow. Life would cease.)

O-sensei taught,

Do not think that you are one who has great problems.

As long as problems are confronted as if they were something outside yourself, you are trapped. You lose your freedom. As in aikido technique, if we sink our whole being into the center of difficulty we unite with it and go beyond it.

Freedom is to enjoy all that you do in such a way that others are also made happier: to serve without any sense of service; constantly to give without any sense of giving. It is to blend with the feeling of others, yet never lose one's own center. For the one who has mastered completely, there is no center: here and now encompasses infinity. In Buddhism, the term *jiyu jizai* is used. It means absolute freedom resulting from the awareness of our nature as the universe.

The final stage is called michi by O-sensei and happiness by Ohsawa. This happiness is not the opposite of unhappiness, nor the happiness that depends on outside circumstances. It is the happiness that comes from knowing true nature. Standing in the center, yet encompassing the periphery, how can contradiction exist? One plays freely with no distinction between the best and the worst. The mind of doubt is gone. A commitment to the way of life occurs spontaneously.

George Ohsawa expressed universal law through seven theorems.[9]

These simple yet deeply significant expressions of nature's laws also express aiki principle.

1. "All things are manifestions of one infinity." Kannagara, the flow of Divine spirit, is the beginningless beginning of all manifestation. Birth, growth, maturity, and death go on endlessly, each ending in a new beginning. All things are born with a certain potential and must return to their origin when that potential, or divine mission, has been fulfilled.

2. "Everything changes." The experience and the one who experiences are always different. The simple and elegant beauty and depth of aikido technique brings fresh joy and insight each day. Sometimes, instead of making progress we appear to go backwards, yet all change is a learning process. Only standing still is not acceptable. Is the master home? If not, who pulls the puppet's strings?

3. "All antagonisms are complementary." Without conflict there is no harmony; without responsibility, no freedom. Without difficulty there would be neither progress nor joy in life. Without ukemi's sincere attack we are not able to study the way of aiki. No one can give you aikido: your progress depends on your own effort and spiritual quality. Your activity and what happens to you are not two different things.

4. "No two things are identical." No two snowflakes are exactly the same. In essence we are the same, yet I am not you and you are not me. Our origin and reality are the same, yet like the snowflakes we are created unequal and different. In the beginning we must learn aikido by imitation; the end product, however, is never the same as the original. Even attempting to copy exactly, individual spiritual substance produces its own aikido, completely unique.

5. "Everything has a front and a back." Irimi (yang) cannot exist without tenkan (yin). These are not two things: they both disappear within the one spirit of Su. They are the back and the front of spiral movement. The success of irimi depends on irimi's including in itself a degree of tenkan. As one's view

becomes clear, the distinction fades. Nothing remains but hara, freely creating.

6. "The bigger the back the bigger the front." Extremes invite their opposite. The person who is too forceful when practicing nage may be open or weak when doing ukemi. One who is too concerned about outward appearances may have a hard time discovering the depth of aikido.

7. "Whatever has a beginning has an end." Each time we reach a new level of understanding we should forget it and go on to the next step. Maintaining beginner's mind, there is no fixed knowing; only continual becoming. Past and future exist only as the present gift of life. When the principle of aikido has become a part of our everyday life, the joy of the movement is always with us. It is only then that we have truly set our feet on the path.

NOTES

Chapter 1. The Origins of Aikido

1. The quotations of Morihei Ueshiba that appear throughout this book, unless otherwise credited, are translated from his *Takemusu Aiki,* transcripts of a series of lectures given for the Byakko Kai religious organization. Similarly, the events of O-sensei's life recounted in this chapter, unless otherwise indicated, are drawn from the biography *Aikido Kaiso Ueshiba Morihei Den,* written by his son, Kisshomaru Ueshiba-doshu, the present head of Honbu Dojo in Japan.
2. Y. Hakeda, Kukai, 17.
3. Quoted in K. Ueshiba, *Aikido Kaiso Ueshiba Morihei Den,* 235.
4. Quoted in Kamata, *Zen to Aikido,* 35.
5. The guardian deity of aikido is Ame no Murakamo Kuki Samuhara Ryuoh Oh Kami, also called Haya Takemusu Oh Kami. In Buddhism this deity is called Hachi Dai Ryu Oh.
6. Although there are several translations of Ueshiba-sensei's poems, I have retranslated this one to capture more of the spirit of the original Japanese.

Chapter 2. The Way of Harmony

1. Sekida, *Zen Training,* Introduction.
2. Whitman, *Leaves of Grass,* 99.
3. Trungpa, *Shambhala,* 126.
4. Capra, *The Tao of Physics,* 23.
5. Hakeda, *Kukai,* 95–96.
6. Capra, *The Tao of Physics,* 146.
7. Lao-tzu, *Tao Te Ching,* trans. D. C. Lau, 58.
8. Matthew 5:39.

9. Reps, *Zen Flesh, Zen Bones,* 39.

10. Lao-tzu, *Tao Te Ching,* trans. Lau, 57.

11. Hee-Jin Kim, in Abé, *Dogen Studies,* 58.

12. Reps, *Zen Flesh, Zen Bones,* 118–19.

Chapter 3. Shinto

1. Mason, *The Meaning of Shinto,* 35.

2. Lao-tzu, *Tao Te Ching,* trans. Wilhelm, 46.

3. Mason, *The Meaning of Shinto,* 98.

4. *Gospel According to Thomas,* 13–15.

Chapter 4. Kototama

1. Dogen, *Shobogenzo,* 32.

2. Hakeda, *Kukai,* 257.

3. Lao-tzu, *Tao Te Ching,* trans. Lau, 61.

4. Capra, *The Tao of Physics,* 12.

5. Kushi, *Macrobiotics and Oriental Medicine,* 36–37.

6. Capra, *The Tao of Physics,* 161.

7. Hakeda, *Kukai,* 234.

8. Mason, *The Meaning of Shinto,* 30, 31.

9. Lao-tzu, *Tao Te Ching,* trans. Lau, 57.

10. Stiskin, *The Looking Glass God,* 89.

11. Matthew 5:13.

12. Ogasawara, *Kototama Hyakushin,* 43–46.

13. Goi, *God and Man,* 20.

14. See Bucke, *Cosmic Consciousness,* passim.

15. Whitman, "Song of Myself," in *Leaves of Grass,* 27.

16. Matthew 12:37, 4:4.

17. *Gospel According to Thomas,* 17.

Chapter 5. One Spirit, Four Souls

1. Taka Ama Hara is the realm of the gods—the center of consciousness and of the infinite universe. Ta is the power of contrast, the first movement of heaven, which created the initial expansion of consciousness. When that expansion has reached its limit it creates Ma,

a perfect sphere of spiritual ki. This is called *tama* or spirit. Ka is the original particle of divine spiritual energy, which, running through the various *tama* and tying them together like a string of pearls, releases the tension of this infinite energy in bursts of great power. It creates the power to move the relative world. Ka and Ma, working together in this way, are *kama*, the boiling pot of word souls from which new consciousness is born. The sound of A is the power of infinite expansion itself. Ha is the power of recognition reaching out to the limits of the universe in order to understand everything. This is the source of human vitality. Ra is the power of circulation. It is spiraling energy that expands, encompasses, and holds all the other energies together.

2. *Dai Nippon Shin Ten,* 13.
3. Manjushri is the Buddhist bodhisattva of wisdom. His sword is said to sever the root of ignorance.

Chapter 6. Three Origins, Eight Powers

1. Hakeda, *Kukai,* 230, 232.
2. Written circa 712 C.E., the *Kojiki* is the most highly regarded ancient mythological history of Japan.
3. In the O-moto teaching, the Eight Powers are combined with their respective deities, yet no branch of Shinto clearly reveals the secret of their corresponding kototama. The relation of kototama to the eight deities here is based on Koji Ogosawara's interpretation of the one hundred deities in the *Kojiki,* as expounded in his *Kototama Hyakushin.*
4. Kakei, *Kannagara no Michi,* 72.
5. Ohsawa, *The Art of Peace,* 106.
6. Kakei, *Kannagara no Michi,* 73.
7. Ibid.
8. Ibid.
9. Matthew 19:17.
10. Deguchi, *Michi no Shiori,* 12.
11. My translation.
12. *I Ching,* 287.
13. Ibid.
14. Govinda, *The Inner Structure of the I-Ching,* 24.

THE SPIRITUAL
FOUNDATIONS OF AIKIDO

178

15, Deshimaru, *The Ring of the Way,* 9.

16. *I Ching,* 287.

17. Ibid.

18. Ibid.

19. Ibid.

20. Ibid.

21. Ibid.

22. *Dai Nippon Shin Ten,* 22.

23. Saito, *Traditional Aikido* 5.38.

24. Quoted in ibid., 5.38.

25. Ogasawara, *Kototama Hyakushin,* 41.

Chapter 7. Practice and Principle

1. Abé, *Dogen Studies,* 76.

2. Ibid., 105.

3. Quoted in Loori, *Mountain Record of Zen Talks,* 47, 49.

4. Deshimaru, *The Ring of the Way,* 81.

5. Hui-neng, in Price and Mou-lam, eds., *The Diamond Sutra and The Sutra of Hui-neng,* 146.

6. Ohsawa, *The Book of Judo,* Introduction.

Chapter 8. The Order of the Universe

1. Prabhavananda and Manchester, eds., *The Upanishads,* 35–36.

2. Kushi, *The Book of Macrobiotics,* 693.

3. Prabhavananda and Manchester, eds., *The Upanishads,* 35–36.

4. Ohsawa, *The Book of Judo,* 2.

5. De Langre, *Do-In,* 10.

6. This translation from Ohsawa's *Book of Judo* differs somewhat from that published in *The Art of Peace.* The publisher of that book (a student of Ohsawa's) and I agree that this translation is more faithful to the spirit of the original.

7. Ohsawa, *The Art of Peace,* 75.

8. Ibid., 23.

9. Ibid., 83–88. These theorems, or principles, form the entire basis of Ohsawa's philosophy and teaching of macrobiotics.

GLOSSARY

In the definitions, words set in *ITALIC SMALL CAPS* are defined elsewhere in the Glossary.

Ai
Love; harmony; mercy and compassion; wisdom.

Aiki
The harmony and order of the universe.

Aiki Bujutsu
Original name of *AIKIDO*.

Aikido
The path of harmony.

Aikidoka
One who practices *AIKIDO*.

Ai nuki
Escaping from a sword battle unharmed and without harming your opponent.

Aiki seishin
AIKI spirit.

Aite
Partner.

Ai uchi
Mutual killing.

Amaterasu Oh Mi Kami
Highest deity of *SHINTO*; the sun goddess, universal spirit.

Amatsu futonorito
Constitution of the paradise, A I E O U; the perfect blending together of physical and spiritual.

Amatsu gami
Highest deity of the heavenly realm.

Amatsu iwasaka
Five levels (seventeen sounds) of a priori existence.

Amatsu kanagi
Way of physicalization, A I U E O.

Amatsu sugaso
Way of spiritualization, A O U E I.

Ame no hashi date
Standing bridge in heaven; the life-will.

Ame no mi hashira
Divine pillar of heaven, A I E O U; subjectivity.

Ame no mi naka nushi
Deity of the center; the void; the KOTOTAMA of U.

Ame no uki hashi
The floating bridge in heaven; the eight powers, Hi Ki Si Ti Yi Ri Mi Ni.

Ana
The name of heaven; a priori consciousness preceding MANA.

Ara hito gami
Human beings with cosmic consciousness said to have lived in the age of the gods.

Aratama
The spirit of fire (YANG); KOTOTAMA of E and Re. Ruler of IKU MUSUBI.

Arigato gozaimasu
Thank you very much.

Asa
Morning.

Asame, trisame, samaye
Same, different, sameness.

Ashi
Leg, foot.

Ashi moto
The space in front of one's feet.

Ashi mimi
(lit., foot-ear); to sense one's partner through the feeling in one's feet.

Atemi
A strike; a blow.

Atman
Individual soul; A.

Aum
Sacred symbol in Sanskrit; primal sound.

Ayakashikone no kami
Deity of the KOTOTAMA Ni; creates human feeling, tenderness, and a sense of nobility.

Banyu aigo
Universal love and compassion; the spirit of protection for all things.

Bokken
Wooden training sword.

Brahman
Hindu god of creation.

Budo (bu)
The spiritual path of the warrior.

Bujutsu
The art of fighting.

Bunrei
Individual spirit; a division of the universal spirit of AMATERASU OH MI KAMI.

Bushido
The way of the samurai; chivalry.

Chi (Ti)
Blood; wisdom; KI.

Chikara
Power (lit., from spirit).

Chikara wo nuku
To drop one's tightness.

Chinkon kishin
Spiritual practice (lit., bringing the soul to peace and returning to God).

Chin Na
Grasping locks (in Japanese, *gyaku te*).

Choku rei
Direct spirit. See *NAOBI*.

Chūdan
Middle-level sword stance; *SEIGAN*.

Dai Nippon Shin Ten
Ancient Shinto text.

Daito ryu jujutsu
The great Eastern way of *JUJUTSU*, supposedly passed down in the emporor lineage to Sokaku Takeda, one of O-sensei's teachers.

Dan
Black-belt rank.

De-ai
Coming out; the beginning of a technique; moment of truth.

Deguchi, Wanisaburo
Founder of O-moto Kyo; spiritual teacher of Morihei Ueshiba-sensei.

Do
TAO; MICHI; a spiritual path.

Do
Trunk of the body.

Dogen
Thirteenth-century founder of Japanese Soto Zen.

Dojo
Place for practice of the way.

Eichi
Wisdom.

Eri tori
Collar grasp.

Fudochi shinmyo ryoku
Doctrine of immovable wisdom by Takuan-zenji.

Fudoshin
Immovable mind.

Fu Hsi
In Chinese mythology, one of the three noble emperors (third millenium B.C.E.) and originator of the eight trigrams of the I-Ching.

Futomani
Universal principle of the *KOTOTAMA*.

Gassho
Formal placing together of the palms of the hands used by Buddhists; a bow.

Gasshuku
Intensive training camp in which students live together for an unbroken period of time.

Geku
Outer shrine at Ise.

Gen
Origin; word.

Genshi
Atom.

Geza no gyo
Training in humility.

Gi
Practice uniform.

Goju suzu gawa
River of the fifty bells (KOTOTAMA).

Gokyo
Fifth teaching.

Gokubi kai
Infinitesmal world of spirit.

Gokui
Enlightenment of BUDO.

Gorin
Five circles.

Gorinhoto
Buddhist gravestone symbolizing five levels.

Go shiki jin
The five different-colored races; the original earthly ancestors of human beings.

Hachiko
Dog memorialized in a statue in Tokyo.

Hachi riki
The Eight Powers.

Hakama
Traditional skirts worn over the GI.

Hanmi
Trianglular stance.

Hanmi handachi
Techniques in which one person is standing and the other sitting.

Hanya shingyo
Buddhist chant (Heart Sutra); one of the main scriptures of Buddhism.

Hara
Center of energy (lit., to spiral outward in eight directions). Defined loosely, hara is situated in the belly; body and mind as one.

Hara ga dekite iru
His HARA is finished, an accomplished man.

Hara de kangaeru
To think with one's HARA.

Hara de yaru
To do from HARA; accomplish technique through the unified power of body, mind, and spirit.

Heishiki-butsu
Second stage (individual) enlightenment in Buddhism.

Hifumi
One, two, three; spirit, mind, and body.

Hiji
Elbow.

Hiji tori
Grasp both elbows from behind.

Himo
Thread.

Himorogi
The thread of will that strings together soul and spirit.

Hinagata
Electromagnetic field or the human soul and spirit.

Hinoki
Japanese cypress.

Hiragana
Japanese cursive alphabet.

Hito
Human being as a fixation of the spirit.

Hitori gami
Individual deity.

Hiza
Knee.

Hokkaido
Northernmost province of Japan.

Honbu Dojo
Main headquarters of aikido.

Ichi nen jo butsu
With one movement of mind, the buddha appears.

Ichi rei shi kon
One spirit four souls.

Iki miya
The human body as a living shrine.

Ikkyo
First teaching; most fundamental technique.

Ikugui no kami
KOTOTAMA of Mi; fills form with *KI* energy.

Iku musubi
KOTOTAMA of Su, A, and Wa; governed by E, the symbol of fire and the triangle. Essence of the animal world.

Ima
Now; the present moment.

Inochi
Motive power of life.

Inori
Prayer.

Irimi
Entering.

Irodama
Spirit of color.

Iroha
Japanese alphabet.

Ise shrine
Main shrine of *SHINTO.*

Ishi
Rock; will.

Ito
String or thread; the invisible will.

Izana
To unite and create paradise.

Izanagi no kami
KOTOTAMA of I.

Izanagi oh kami
I and Wi as one; the divine ancestors of human beings in Japanese mythology. Pure love and perfect wisdom.

Izanami no kami
KOTOTAMA of Wi.

Izunome no mikoto
Perfect balance of *YIN* and *YANG* in the universe.

Jiku
Axis (*ji* is time; *ku* is space).

Jiriki
Self-power.

Jiyu jizai
Absolute freedom resulting from awareness of one's own nature as the universe itself; a Buddhist term.

Jo
Wooden training staff.

Judo
Martial art of self-defense founded by Jigoro Kano.

Jujutsu
Ju, yielding; *jutsu*, art technique. Any of 725 officially documented systems of unarmed combat.

Jyaki
Evil feeling.

Kado matsu
Pine wreath—symbolizing waiting—placed on house doors before the new year.

Kagami
Mirror; to see oneself through the eyes of God.

Kagura mai
Dance of the gods.

Kaiten nage
Rotating throw.

Kakurigami
Hidden deity.

Kamae
Stance.

Kami
SHINTO deity; universal energy.

Kami musubi no kami
Deity of objective consciousness.

Kamiwaza
Inspired, divine technique; techniques using universal principle and spiritual power.

Kangaeru
To think (lit., returning to God).

Kanji
Japanese writing system; a single character in that system.

Kannagara no michi
Way of the gods; divine flow of God-mind.

Kannon
Highest deity in the Buddhist pantheon. Male and female as one.

Kano Jigoro
Founder of *JUDO*.

Karada
Body.

Kashima shin ryu
Divinely inspired sword style of Deer Island, possibly the first formalized sword school in Japan. One of several ancient sword styles studied by O-sensei.

Kata
Prescribed sequence of movements for studying the principles of martial arts. Shoulder (*kata tori* is "shoulder grasp").

Katakana
Japanese block-letter alphabet.

Katana
Japanese long-sword.

Katate tori
One-hand grasp of a partner's wrist.

Katsu hayabi
Instantaneous; beyond time and space.

Katsujin ken
The way of winning a sword battle without harming the opponent.

Kawa wa taezu nagareru, shikamo
The river flows constantly, yet it changes not. One must act in the moment.

Kayabuki
Thatched roof.

Kazotama
Spirit of numbers.

Keiko
Practice; to make one's mind together with that of the ancient masters.

Kensho
One's first experience of enlightenment.

Kesa giri
A diagonal sword-cut to the neck or chest.

Ki
Spiritual energy; mind; feeling.

Ki-ai
Release of physical and spiritual power in the form of a shout. It was said in ancient times that this power, developed properly, could bring down a bird in flight.

Kimono
Japanese traditional dress.

Ki-musubi
Unifying; tying together *KI* or feeling.

Kitai
Spiritual *(KI)* body; advanced aikido method in which the partner is touched hardly at all.

Koan
Zen paradox (or "public example") designed to lead the mind beyond conceptual thought.

Kobo-daishi
See *KUKAI*.

Kohai
Junior student.

Kojiki
Book of ancient happenings *(SHINTO)*.

Kokyu
Breath (expansion and contraction).

Kokyu ho
The way (law) of breath; the most fundamental exercise of aikido.

Kokyu nage
A throw executed by rhythm and *KI* extension alone.

Kokyu ryoku
The power of *KOKYU.*

Koryu
Old or ancient style.

Kongo
Mandala of *SHINGON* Buddhism.

Kosa tori
Cross-hand grasp.

Koshi
Hips.

Koshi nage
Hip throw.

Koshi ga suwaru
To be well grounded; stable
(lit., the hips sit down).

Kote gaeshi
Return-the-wrist-throw.

Koto
Word.

Kototama
Word souls.

Ku
The sky; emptiness.

Kui aratameru
To amend one's ways.

Kukai
Buddhist teacher; ninth-century
founder of the Shingon school. His
honorific title is Kobo-daishi.

Kumi tachi
Two-person sword practice.

Kuni no mi hashira
Divine pillar of earth (objectivity);
KOTOTAMA of Wa Wi We Wo Wu.

Kurai
Position.

Kurai dachi
Sword movement that exemplifies
IKKYO, the first principle of aikido.

Kuro obi
Black belt (Kuro obi kai is a black
belt-seminar).

Kushi
A skewer.

Kushi tama
KOTOTAMA of I.

Ku soku ze shiki, shiki soku ze ku.
Emptiness is form and form is
emptiness.

Kyu
White-belt rank.

Ma
See *MAKOTO.*

Ma-ai
Distance; correct distance and
timing.

Mahavairochana Dharmakaya
Body of the universe; Great Sun
Buddha.

Magatama
Symbol of the energy of
materialization; beads.

Mahayana
The so-called great vehicle of Buddhism; the path of salvation for all (as distinct from the Hinayana, which from a Mahayana viewpoint is the path of individual liberation).

Makoto
True mind; sincerity; honesty.

Mana
Manna; bread; the true word or divine nourishment.

Manjushri
Buddhist bodhisattva of wisdom.

Mantra
Syllable or verse to be repeated; a form of meditation.

Maruten
A point within a circle; the symbol of the KOTOTAMA of Su.

Matsu
As a noun, *pine tree*; as a verb, *to wait*.

Me
Eyes.

Men tsuki
Punch to the face.

Michi
The way of life; divine knowledge.

Michiru
To be full; complete; thrive.

Miizu
Divine authority.

Mikoto
Deity in the flesh; manifestation of MAKOTO.

Mikotoha
Wave of life energy.

Misogi
Purification; scraping off physical and spiritual pollution.

Mitama
Spirit and soul.

Mitama migaki
To polish the soul; to raise intuitive judgment.

Mitama shizume
Bringing the soul to peace through activity.

Miyamoto, Musashi
Famous Japanese swordsman.

Motogaeri
To return to one's spiritual origin.

Mu
The invisible energy world.

Mudra
Bodily posture or gesture, usually made with the hands.

Mujushin
The mind of no abode.

Mune
Chest (*mune tsuki* is a straight punch to the solar plexus).

Mushin
Mind without attachment or ego.

Musubi
Unifying; tying together YIN and YANG.

Muso Genri
The unique principle, YIN-YANG.

Myo
Unique, marvelous mystery of the universe.

Nage
A throw; one who throws.

Naiku
Inner shrine at *ISE*.

Nanji
Polite term for *you*.

Nakayima (Nakaima)
Here and now.

Naobi
Direct and corrective spirit; *CHOKU REI*; *KOTOTAMA* of Su and U.

Nigen
Two origins, *YIN* and *YANG*.

Nigi (Nigiwau)
To flourish; prosper; thrive.

Nigitama
Spirit of water (O); ruler of *TARU MUSUBI*.

Nikkyo
Second teaching; showing *YIN* as opposed to *YANG*.

Nurutama
Sleeping soul; another name for *SAKITAMA*.

Nyoi
The so-called wish-fulfilling scepter of Buddhism and Taoism.

Ohotonobe no kami
KOTOTAMA of Ri. Makes consciousness effective.

Ohotonoji no kami
KOTOTAMA of Si. Produces human consciousness and spiritual feeling.

Okugi
Highest or secret teaching.

Omoiyari
An attitude of concern for the feelings of others.

Omotaru no kami
KOTOTAMA of Hi. Provides spiritual power.

Omote
Front; front of the *DOJO*; basic *(YANG)* technique in which direct confrontation is practiced.

Omoto-kyo
SHINTO sect founded by Deguchi Wanisaburo, O-sensei's spiritual teacher (lit., teaching of the great origin).

Oh Kuni Tama Oh Kuni Nushi
Deity of happiness and spiritual wealth.

Omou
To think; instinctive mind.

Onegai shimasu
Request for practice or instruction.

O-sensei
Great teacher.

Otamaguchi
A *SHINTO* offering made to the gods; symbol of One Spirit, Four Souls.

Otodama
Spirit of sound.

Parasabda
Primal sound in the Indian
(Sanskrit) tradition; *AUM.*

Potchi
The first spark of life and
consciousness; the point at the
center of the circle in the symbol
for Su.

Randori
Multiple-opponent attack.

Rashisa
Suchness; being just what you are.

Rei
Formality; politeness; a bow; spirit.

Reigan
Spiritual vision; third eye.

Reigi saho
Formality; etiquette.

Reiso joka
Raising one's spiritual level.

Renshu
Practice through repetition.

Risshin
Vertical mind; will.

Rokkon shojo
To purify the six organs of the body.

Ryobu
Dual mandala.

Ryote tori
Using both hands, grasping each of
the opponent's wrists.

Sa
Difference.

Sakarau
To oppose or go against.

Sakebu
To shout.

Sakaeru
To prosper.

Sakeru
To break through.

Sakitama
KOTOTAMA of A; ruler of
TAMATSUME MUSUBI.

Saku
To blossom.

Sakurazawa, Yukikazu
George Ohsawa, founder of the
macrobiotic movement.

Samadhi
Trancelike state beyond all dualism.

Sangen
Three Origins.

Sanin
See *YAMAKAGE.*

Sankyo
Third teaching; spiral movement
combined with *YIN-YANG*
opposition.

Sarutahiko Ohkami
Pioneer deity of justice and
righteousness, head of all earthly
KAMI.

Satori
Zen term for enlightenment.

Satsujin ken
Way of killing with a sword.

Seigan
Middle-level *(CHUDAN)* sword stance; correct way of seeing; correct view.

Seiza
Formal sitting or kneeling posture; sitting on the heels.

Senpai
Senior student.

Sensei
Teacher (lit., first-born).

Sengu Shiki
Rebuilding of *ISE SHRINE* every twenty years.

Senshu no Kannon
KANNON of one thousand arms.

Sente
To take initiative.

Senten
Before heaven; *ANA*.

Shi
The spiritual atom; ruler of the *KOTOTAMA*.

Shido
Spiritual path of the warrior.

Shiho
Four directions; salt; human essence.

Shiho nage
Four-directions throw.

Shikko
Knee-walking; *SUWARI WAZA*.

Shime
A choke or tight grasp of the whole body.

Shimenawa
Braided rope connecting the two sides of the gate to a *SHINTO* shrine. It symbolizes the connection between subjective and objective consciousness.

Shin
Heart; mind; spirit; center; core; God.

Shinkage
Name of a sword style.

Shingon Mikkyo
Esoteric Buddhism.

Shinjin
True heart, true mind (a Buddhist term created by *SHINRAN*).

Shin nyo
The likeness of truth.

Shinran
Founder of the Buddhist Nichiren sect (1222–82).

Shinto
The way of the gods. Japanese national religion and original government.

Shinshin toitsu
Body-mind unification.

Shireri (shiru)
To know.

Shobu
Martial way of wisdom.

Shoshin
Beginner's mind.

Shomen
The front of the dojo, where the shrine is located.

Shomen uchi
A direct strike to the face or top of the head.

Shugendo
Esoteric mountain religion.

Shugyo
Spiritual training or polishing.

Su
Ruler of the *KOTOTAMA; NAOBI; CHOKUREI;* creator god of the universe.

Suberu
To govern or control; to slide; *KOTOTAMA* that creates the spiraling essence of nature's process.

Suburi
Individual sword practice in which the same stroke is continuously repeated.

Suhiji no Kami
Deity that creates the ability to weather difficulties; *KOTOTAMA* of Yi.

Suki
An opening or weak point.

Sumera no Mikoto
Original name for the Japanese emperor, who is now called *TENNO.*

Sunao
One who knows *MAKOTO* (lit., to harmonize with the *KOTOTAMA* of Su).

Sun Tsu
Author of *The Art of War.*

Susa no Wo no Mikoto
Brother of *AMATERASU OH MI KAMI;* deity of science, materialization, and *BUDO.* His duty is to bring the light of the spirit back into the world (*ama no iwato biraki*).

Suwari waza
Practicing on one's knees.

Suzuki, Daisetsu
Japanese scholar and interpreter of Zen for the West.

Tabi
Traditional Japanese socks, similar to a slipper, worn with *KIMONO.*

Tachi
Long Japanese sword; wisdom; judgment. As a verb, to cut off or sever.

Tachi tori
Taking away the sword.

Tada
Just; only.

Tai atari
Whole-body connection.

Tai Jutsu
Bare-handed techniques.

Taikyoku
Infinity; the absolute.

Taizo
The lower world.

Taizo-butsu
See *TAMATSUME MUSUBI*.

Taka ama hara
The high heavenly plain; the universe; spiritual center.

Takami Musubi no Kami
Deity of subjective consciousness.

Takeda, Sokaku
Founder of Daito-ryu jujutsu.

Takemusubi
Creative energy of the universe.

Takemusubi aiki
An early name for *AIKIDO*.

Takuan-zenji
Sixteenth-century Zen master; teacher of *MIYAMOTO MUSASHI*.

Tama
Precious stones; spirit.

Tamashii
Human spirit and soul.

Tamatsume musubi
One Spirit, Four Souls and Eight Powers functioning harmoniously together; divided spirit of *AMATERASU OH MI KAMI*; symbolized by the earth and the square; essence of the mineral world, ruled by *KOTOTAMA* of Ai.

Tanden
HARA; burning place or energy center.

Tanden no ichi
One point; center of the physical *HARA*.

Tanren
Same as *RENSHU*.

Tanto
Wooden practice knife.

Tanto tori
Taking away the knife.

Tao
KANNAGARA; MICHI.

Tao Te Ching
Taoist work of five thousand pictograms attributed to Lao-tzu; *Book of the Way*.

Tariru
Sufficient; enough.

Taru musubi
KOTOTAMA of E and O; symbol of water and the circle; essence of the vegetable world.

Tatsu
To stand.

Tatsu jin
A master of *BUDO* (lit., one who has stood up).

Tariki
Other power (compare with *JIRIKI*).

Te
Hand.

Tegatana
Hand blade.

Ten
A point; heaven.

Tenchi nage
Heaven-earth throw.

Tenkan
A pivot to dissipate an opponent's force.

To
Transparency; super-speed; breaking through to clarity.

Tori (dori)
A grasp.

Torii
The gate passed through to enter a *SHINTO* shrine.

Toru
To remove or take away.

Toyoke no oh mi kami
God of the earth.

Tsu
KOTOTAMA of pushing strongly toward materialization.

Tsukasatoru
As a verb, *to take care of.*

Tsuki
A thrust; a straight punch.

Tsuki Yomi no Kami
Brother of *AMATERASU OH MI KAMI;* god of philosophy and religion.

Tsumi
Accumulation; defilement.

Tsunugui no kami
KOTOTAMA of Ki; creates form.

Tsurugi
Japanese sword. As a verb, to connect or tie together spiritual energy.

Ubusuna
SHINTO deity of birth and production.

Uchi
A strike.

Uchi deshi
Live-in student or apprentice.

Uchi tachi
Person who attacks (sword).

Uchi wa fuku, oni wa soto
Folk chant: Out with the goblin and in with happiness.

Uchu
The universe.

Uhijini no Kami
Deity of opposition and contradiction; *KOTOTAMA* of Ti.

Uji bashi
Bridge where universal law presides.

Uke
Person who receives the attack.

Ukemi
Art of receiving, falling, and moving in such a way as to have no openings where one could be attacked.

Uke tachi
Person who receives the attack (sword).

Umu
To give birth.

Ura
Back or reverse side *(YIN)*.
Advanced techniques in which the
attack is not met directly but is
avoided by a *TENKAN* movement.

Utsushiyo
The manifest (reflected) world.

Uzu
Spiral; comes from U-Su the
KOTOTAMA of direct spirit.

Ware
Myself.

Waza
Technique.

Yagyu, Munenori
Head of the Yagyu Shinkage school
of swordsmanship.

Yagyu Shinkage ryu
Sword style passed down in the
Yagyu family. Strong influence on
O-sensei's training.

Yamakage
Sanin sect of *SHINTO.*

Yang
Centrifugal force, light, male, spirit,
heaven.

Yata
Pushing outward in all directions;
returning directly to infinity. See
KAGAMI (mirror of yata).

Yin
Centripetal force, darkness, female,
body, earth.

Yin-yang
Universal law; polarity.

Yokomen uchi
A diagonal strike to the side of the
head.

Yonkyo
Fourth teaching.

Yu
Hot water (Iu); to speak; courage.

Yudansha
Black-belt holder.

Zanshin
Remaining mind; unbroken
concentration.

BIBLIOGRAPHY

Abé, Masao. *Dogen Studies*. Honolulu: University of Hawaii Press, 1986.

Aihara, Herman. *Learning from Salmon*. Oroville, Calif.: Ohsawa Pub., 1980.

Bucke, Richard. *Cosmic Consciousness*. New York: Dutton, 1969.

Capra, Fritjov. *The Tao of Physics*. Boston: Shambhala, 1991.

Dai Nippon Shin Ten. Translated by Kiyoshi Mizutani. Nagoya, Japan, 1907.

Deguchi, Wanisaburo. *Michi no Shiori*. Tokyo: O-moto Kyo, 1948.

De Langre, Jack. *Do-In*. Rev. ed. Vol. 1. Magalia, Calif.: Happiness Press, 1990.

Deshimaru, T. *The Ring of the Way*. New York: Dutton, 1983.

Dogen Zenji. *Shobogenzo*. Translated by Thomas Cleary. Honolulu: University of Hawaii Press, 1986.

Durckheim, Karlfried. *Hara*. London: Allen & Unwin, 1962.

Erasmus, D. *In Praise of Folly*. London: Penguin Classics, 1971.

Goi, M. *God and Man*. Tokyo: Byakko Kai, 1953.

Gospel According to Thomas. Edited by E. J. Brill. New York: Harper & Row, 1959.

Govinda, Lama Anagarika. *The Inner Structure of the I-Ching*. New York: Wheelwright Press, 1981.

Hakeda, Y. *Kukai*. New York: Columbia University Press, 1972.

I Ching: Book of Changes. New York: Pantheon, 1950.

Kakei, Katsuhiko. *Kannagara no Michi*. Tokyo: Kogakukan, 1926.

Kamata, Shigeo. *Zen to Aikido*. Tokyo: Hakujusha, 1984.

———. *Zen to Ken no Gokui*. Tokyo: Hakujusha, 1962.

Kojiki, Nihon Shoki. Translated by Takehiko Fukunaga. Tokyo: Nihon Koten Bunko, 1934.

Kushi, Michio. *The Book of Macrobiotics*. New York: Japan Pub., 1977.

———. *Macrobiotics and Oriental Medicine*. New York: Japan Pub., 1991.

————. *On the Greater View*. New York: Avery, 1986.

————. *The Origin and Destiny of Man*. Boston: East-West, 1971.

Lao-tzu. *Tao Te Ching*. Translated by D. C. Lau. Middlesex, England: Penguin Books, 1963.

————. *Tao Te Ching*. Translated by Mitchell. New York: Harper Perennial, 1991.

————. *Tao Te Ching*. Translated by Richard Wilhelm. London: Arkana, 1985.

Loori, J. Daido. *Mountain Record of Zen Talks*. New York: Dharma Communications, 1992.

Mason, James. *The Meaning of Shinto*. New York: Dutton, 1935.

Nakazono, M. *The Kototama Principle*. Santa Fe, N.M.: Kototama Institute, 1983.

Ogasawara, Koji. *Kototama Hyakushin*. Tokyo: Toyokan, 1969.

Ohsawa, George. *The Art of Peace*. Translated by William Gleason. Oroville, Calif.: Ohsawa Foundation, 1990.

————. *The Book of Judo*. Tokyo: Nihon, 1952.

————. *Health and Happiness*. Oroville, Calif.: Ohsawa Foundation, 1971.

Okada, S. *Mahikari*. Tokyo: Mahikari Kyo, 1972.

Omori, Sogen. *Ken to Zen*. Tokyo, 1972.

Prabhavananda, Swami, and Frederick Manchester, eds. *The Upanishads*. New York: Mentor Classic, 1948.

Price, A. F., and Wong Mou-lam, eds. *The Diamond Sutra and The Sutra of Hui-neng*. Boston: Shambhala, 1990.

Reps, Paul. *Zen Flesh, Zen Bones*. New York: Doubleday, 1961.

Revised English Bible. Cambridge: Oxford University Press, 1989.

Saito, Morihiro. *Traditional Aikido*. Vol. 5. Tokyo: Minato Research, 1976.

Sekida, Katsuki. *Zen Training*. New York: Weatherhill, 1985.

Stiskin, Nahum. *The Looking Glass God*. Boston: Autumn Press, 1972.

Sun-tzu. *The Art of War*. Translated by Thomas Cleary. Boston: Shambhala, 1988.

Suzuki, S. *Zen Mind, Beginner's Mind*. New York: Weatherhill, 1970.

Trungpa, Chögyam. *Shambhala: The Sacred Path of the Warrior*. Boston: Shambhala, 1988.

Ueshiba, Kisshomaru. *Aikido Kaiso Ueshiba Morihei Den*. Tokyo: Kodansha, 1977.

Ueshiba, Morihei. *The Art of Peace*. Translated by John Stevens. Boston: Shambhala, 1992.

———. *Budo Renshu*. Tokyo: Minato Research, 1978.

———. *Takemusu Aiki*. Tokyo: Byakko Kai, 1977.

Whitman, Walt. *Leaves of Grass*. 1855. New York: Viking Press, 1959.

Yamakage, M. *Koki Hitsuden*. Tokyo: Kasumigaseki, 1971.

———. *Shinto no Gendaiteki Kaishaku*. Tokyo: Kasumigaseki, 1962.

Yamamoto, Yukitaka. *Way of the Kami*. Stockton, Calif.: Tsubaki America, 1987.

INDEX